PERFECT ENGLISH
Small and Beautiful

PERFECT ENGLISH
Small and Beautiful

ROS BYAM SHAW

photography by

ANTONY CROLLA

RYLAND PETERS & SMALL
LONDON • NEW YORK

To Max, Clementine, Jude and Eva

Senior designer Toni Kay
Senior commissioning editor Annabel Morgan
Location research Jess Walton
Production manager Gordana Simakovic
Creative director Leslie Harrington

First published in 2025 by
Ryland Peters & Small
20–21 Jockey's Fields
London WC1R 4BW
and
1452 Davis Bugg Road
Warrenton, NC 27589
www.rylandpeters.com

10 9 8 7 6 5 4 3 2 1

ISBN 978-1-78879-669-9

FSC
MIX
Paper | Supporting
responsible forestry
FSC® C106563
www.fsc.org

A CIP record for this book is available
from the British Library.

Library of Congress CIP data
has been applied for.

Printed and bound
in China

CONTENTS

INTRODUCTION

'Small' and 'beautiful' are relative terms. My Granny, at just over five feet/152 cm tall, was both to me, and 'Small' was her family nickname, but in another age it might have been 'Tall'. I have been particularly conscious of comparative size in terms of square footage while writing this book. Most of the homes shown here are less than 1,000 square feet/92 square metres; some a lot less, some a little more. And just under 1,000 square feet/92 square metres is the size of the average new-build house in the UK. So while I may be able to justify the 'Beauty' of the title, you might question its accompanying adjective.

AVERAGE HOUSES DON'T OFTEN FEATURE in coffee-table books, particularly not ones devoted to a style that is more often associated with rectories and manor houses. But the idea for this book came to me when I clocked that the last three homes I had written about were all decidedly bijou. Then, thinking back over all the hundreds of interiors I have visited and described in a forty-year career, I realized that the more modest ones belonging to people without big budgets had the most appeal. King of English country house decorating John Fowler was a dab hand at draping huge windows and grouping furniture in the vast drawing rooms of stately homes, but his most memorable and charming rooms are those of the miniature hunting lodge he decked out for himself. We can all create glorious interiors without the luxury of grand proportions.

There is proof enough in the following pages that limited floor space doesn't have to limit ambition. The old adage that a large piece of furniture makes a little room feel bigger is put into practice time and again, with four-poster beds that have to be edged around, handsome sofas that stretch from wall to wall and oil paintings you might expect to see hanging in a grand dining room rather than a cottage parlour. Every house and flat here has a strong visual character as expressive and creative as could be achieved in any palace or mansion.

Of course there are compromises in a small home. Certain pieces of furniture cannot be coaxed up a tight staircase. Ceiling height can dictate your choice of grandfather clock. A grand piano is inevitably impractical. Some of the homeowners featured on these pages freely admit that they are bursting at the seams. Books and pictures are the most likely possessions to spill over onto floors and stairs. But all appreciate that there are also positive advantages. Guy Marshall enjoys the fact that he can sit in a corner and stretch his feet across to warm them at the fire on the other side of his living room. Decorator Libby Lord points out that you can feel free to experiment, as mistakes are not quite as expensive. Everyone agrees that limited space forces you to prioritize and to choose carefully and thoughtfully what you do and don't keep. While all these owners would describe themselves as 'collectors', by necessity their collections are constantly refined. I couldn't help noticing that these are people who dress particularly well despite having minimal wardrobes.

On a practical level, plenty of storage is paramount in a small home – using every nook, cranny, corner, back-of-door, over-door, under-stairs and under-the-bed space available, and remembering that a single cupboard can hide a disparate variety of things both large and small. Simon Martin has one on his landing that contains his washing machine, iron, ironing board and clothes airer with a row of jackets hanging above them, while Kevin Oliver's kitchen spices are kept in a rack attached to the inside of the boiler cupboard door. Both Will Le Clerc and Guy Marshall have floor-to-ceiling pictures hanging on their staircases and Guy also uses his to stack books. In other space-saving tricks, Libby Lord had her bedroom doors rehung so they open outwards onto the landing instead of into the room, and many spaces in these little homes are divided by a curtain instead of a door as a means to gain a bit of extra wall.

By coincidence, I signed up to write this book just before we made the decision to move from our large house to one that is a fraction of the size. I cannot pretend I have found this an easy adjustment. I too am a collector and, as a slave to Parkinson's Law, find that in the last twenty-three years I have somehow managed to fill large rooms, multiple cupboards and an extensive attic, plus a workshop, a walk-in larder and several outbuildings with stuff. Winnowing out the best and most beloved has proved by turns exhilarating and exhausting. And although I have felt short of time, writing about these people and their homes has been a constant source of inspiration and delight. I have also come to believe that small will be beautiful.

MATERIAL GAINS

'It was a classic downsize,' says Ali Kelsey of her move three years ago to a farmworker's cottage of just 100 square metres/1,076 square feet from a thatched mill house more than three times as large. It's a move that might have sparked sympathy among well-heeled friends with sizeable drawing rooms. Instead, the combination of prettiness, comfort, convenience and economy she has created is more likely to prompt sighs of envy. 'I can still just about squeeze in all four of my grown-up boys when they come to stay, and we had ten round the table at Christmas.'

NOT EVERYONE WOULD HAVE SEEN the potential. The cottage is one of a pair, built in 1945. Plastic windows had replaced the old multi-pane casements, but the original layout hadn't changed and there was no bathroom, just a loo squeezed onto the tiny landing, and a downstairs cloakroom with a cramped corner shower and washbasin. The front door opened onto a steep staircase with the living room on the left, a breakfast room on the right and a kitchen beyond it. Upstairs there were three bedrooms.

What the house lacked in charm it made up for with its location, sitting on a rise above the junction of two lanes in rural Somerset. From here you can look past a 400-year-old oak tree down towards the honey-coloured stone and thatch of the old farmhouse and

ABOVE LEFT The cottage is one of a pair built in the mid-1940s on raised ground above the junction of two narrow lanes. The kitchen and living-room windows at the front face west and Ali says the views of sunsets are spectacular.

LEFT Originally, the front door opened onto a walled-in staircase with a door into the dining room. The cottages are so sturdily built that it took four men a day to take the wall down and open up the space into what is now the kitchen.

OPPOSITE A local joiner made the kitchen cupboards, which are painted in Farrow & Ball Pigeon, and glued the floorboards, covered with Farrow & Ball Blue Gray, over the old concrete flooring. The blinds are in Mortfontaine by Pierre Frey.

THIS PAGE The kitchen walls are lined with matchboard panelling painted in Farrow & Ball Lime White, here a background for an early 20th-century landscape by Reginald Tilbrook, which Ali bought at auction, and a selection of favourite postcards and photographs. The pot of wooden spoons sits just to the left of the cooker.

ABOVE The wall between the kitchen at the front and the room behind it that was originally the kitchen has been knocked through to make a wide opening linking it with the new dining area. There is a view through to the downstairs loo, which has a Robert Kime wallpaper.

across its gardens, hedges and fields. 'I already knew these cottages, as our old house is not far from here and I used to walk past them with the dogs,' says Ali. 'The couple who were selling were in their seventies and the husband said to me that when he sat in his armchair and looked out of the front window, he would think to himself, 'If that is what heaven looks like, I don't mind dying.'

The view hasn't changed but, looking from the outside in, pretty much everything else has. By knocking down the wall that hemmed in one side of the staircase and the wall between the breakfast room and

kitchen, and taking out the larder that separated the cooking area from the living room, Ali has created an open, U-shaped space that wraps around the staircase. The front door now opens into the kitchen, once the breakfast room, and extends into the former kitchen, where bench seating hugs three sides of the space under a new, larger window. 'I needed to maximize seating around the table, and this seemed the best way to do it,' says Ali. The downstairs shower has been replaced by a lavatory and bedroom three has become a bathroom. Every plastic window has been exchanged for timber – still double-glazed, but much better looking.

Like all successful rearrangements, it feels right, obvious even. 'I could see immediately what had to be done,' says Ali. 'And I already knew local people who could help, particularly Martyn Male, who is a brilliant carpenter and had done a lot of work on my previous house. He made all the new windows on site, and the kitchen and bookshelves, he repurposed old doors and found a way to glue pine planks onto the concrete floors so that I could have the painted wooden floors I wanted. Victoria Bletsoe is a wonderful seamstress and made the curtains, cushions, window seats and bed valances. Between them, there isn't much that Martyn and Victoria didn't do, aside from plumbing and electrics.'

PAGES 14–15 The area now filled by the dining table was once the kitchen and had a single, small window. Thanks to a pair of new, much bigger windows, the space is now flooded with light. Bench seating maximizes the number of people the table can accommodate. The bench cushions and the blinds are in Bowood by Colefax and Fowler, made from a pair of curtains Ali bought on eBay. The group portrait of Ali's four sons is by Rosanna Chittenden.

LEFT In the living room, the George Smith sofa is upholstered in a Colefax and Fowler stripe and all the cushions are made from antique textiles. An antique suzani embroidery bought in Istanbul covers the upholstered stool.

OPPOSITE The French doors that open from the living room into the garden are also new. Only the beams in the ceiling betray that this open space was once divided into smaller rooms. The painting above the sideboard is *Siberian Fairytale* by Yuri Yegorov, a mid-20th century Ukrainian artist, and was bought by Ali many years ago when she spotted it from the window of her London flat hanging in an art gallery across the road.

RIGHT On the right of the living-room fireplace, a bust of Cicero found in a Brighton junk shop 30 years ago takes centre stage in front of a panel of antique crewel work embroidery bought more recently at a textiles fair. Another old suzani from Istanbul is draped over the back of the armchair.

BELOW Ali has a passion for antique textiles and finds creative ways to use them, whether as borders for curtains, to make cushions or upholster chairs. These are pieces awaiting reinvention.

Ali began her career in the London art world, working for the Tate and Anthony d'Offay before relocating to Somerset. 'I became quite disillusioned with it – ridiculous amounts of money being bandied around often for works of little intrinsic merit.' She has since turned to the world of decorating. In addition to her talent for reorganizing space, she has a love of textiles, a nose for finding them at bargain prices and an eye for mixing colour and pattern.

Victoria's handiwork can be seen everywhere, from the gingham front-door curtain with its appliquéd embroidery to the glorious array of cushions, many of them made using pieces

THIS PAGE Walls and panelling up the stairs are painted in Mizzle by Farrow & Ball, and the stair runner is from Roger Oates. At the top of the stairs is Ali's bedroom on the left, seen here through the door.

ABOVE AND LEFT In the main bedroom, the bed sits in front of the window and faces a window opposite that looks over the back garden. Walls are Welmish Blew by Edward Bulmer, the blind is in a Kathryn Ireland fabric bought on eBay and the headboard and armchair are both upholstered in fabrics by Raoul Textiles. Above the chest of drawers is a tiled panel and on it is a matching vase, both bought in Istanbul.

RIGHT Ali made the third bedroom into a bathroom, with walls painted in Mizzle by Farrow & Ball and curtains in Paradise from Bennison. The floorboards are painted in Farrow & Ball Slipper Satin, as in the main bedroom.

LEFT AND ABOVE The spare bedroom has walls in Farrow & Ball Dix Blue and a pair of vintage embroidered bedcovers on the twin beds, matched with valances and headboards in a gingham check. The cushions are Raoul Textiles, and the armchair is for Ali to sit in when she becomes a grandparent and reads bedtime stories. of wool work found by Ali at antique textiles fairs. A curtain hanging on the landing incorporates a panel of old crewel work, and the window-seat cushions, in Colefax and Fowler chintz, were cut from a pair of second-hand curtains. Pieces of early Victorian embroidery folded under a console table in the sitting room await a new life. 'I might use one as a pelmet,' says Ali. Like all natural decorators, she considers her house a work in progress, and you feel sure it will only get prettier.

INNER BEAUTY

This is one of the smallest of the 12 homes in this book and was its inspiration. Its unremarkable, two-storey, red-brick facade on the back street of a quiet town in north Shropshire is a scant 3.5 metres/11½ feet wide. It belongs to furniture restorer Guy Marshall, and he has filled the two downstairs rooms and one upstairs bedroom with a collection of Georgian furniture, china, clocks, paintings and ornaments that would be the envy of the owner of many a large country house. Stepping through his front door is like finding treasure in a shoebox.

JUST AFTER I MOVED IN, a lady in her eighties knocked on the door,' he says. 'She had been brought up here with her parents and brother, before the kitchen and shower room were built on at the back, when it was still a one-up-one-down slum with holes in the floorboards and a privy in the yard. Her father was a cobbler and worked in a windowless cellar under the living room. It brought tears to her eyes to see it made so comfortable.'

Guy's idea of comfort is not everyone's. When he bought the house 12 years ago it had double glazing, fitted carpets, central heating and a new fitted kitchen. All have been jettisoned, the windows in favour of single-glazed sashes, the carpet replaced by a patchwork layering of worn antique rugs, the radiators removed

ABOVE LEFT The cottage is at the end of a terrace and has been extended into its backyard, so the front door is now at the side beneath the rampaging wisteria. The original front door on the street is no longer in use.

LEFT Narrow wooden stairs rise to the left from just behind the new front door and are used as a bookcase, while the walls are a tight tessellation of 18th-century prints and engravings. To the right is the entrance to the kitchen.

OPPOSITE As well as replacing the later windows with wooden sashes, Guy dismantled the central heating and took out all the radiators. He made a fire surround for an old register grate in the living room, and this is now his only source of heating in the house.

OPPOSITE Georgian wing chairs with stripy slipcovers are tucked into the corners of the living room opposite the fireplace on either side of a table that holds an exquisite 18th-century creamware jug among other treasures. The corner cabinet is full of 18th-century creamware and pearlware.

in favour of an open fire. 'The radiators took up too much space', he says, 'and the advantage of a small room is that I can sit in the corner and stretch my legs across to toast my toes.'

As for the kitchen, he removed it 'in stages' as pieces of antique furniture edged it out. Where once there was chipboard and plastic there are now two chinoiserie corner cupboards, an oak hanging cupboard, a grandfather clock with a moon face dial, a serpentine sideboard, a mahogany chest of drawers, a drop-leaf table, a tripod table and three dining chairs, all 18th century. The last man standing from its previous incarnation is the stainless-steel sink, although the cupboard doors beneath have been replaced with curtains made from antique fabric. Guy cooks on a vintage Baby Belling on which he also boils water in a copper kettle for tea. Next to it is an electric toaster. 'I often heat up a pie for dinner, but I have been known to cook a pheasant for friends' – presumably not a very fat one.

ABOVE The early 18th-century grandfather clock was one of two non-negotiable pieces of furniture there had to be space for, the other being the four-poster bed. Had the ceiling been an inch lower, Guy would not have bought the house.

PAGES 28–29 To the right of the fireplace, a mahogany bookcase supports an arrangement of 18th-century pieces: a pair of silver candlesticks, a pair of tole urns and a clock. Although the room is full, everything is so beautifully grouped and placed that the effect is elegant rather than cluttered.

LEFT A bureau desk slots perfectly into the recess to the left of the living-room fireplace with above it an arrangement of perfect symmetry: a splendid pair of Staffordshire lions flanking the lamp and a collection of portrait miniatures either side of the mirror.

OPPOSITE The living room narrows where the staircase rises behind the wall on the right. The space beyond the door is a later extension, now housing the kitchen – or what remains of it – and a shower room. Guy has covered the concrete floor with a layering of antique rugs.

PAGES 32–33 Looking from the kitchen sink back through the house to the front window in the living room, the tiny hall and staircase are to the left. When Guy bought the house, this space was filled by a fitted kitchen that he removed to make space for a late 18th-century mahogany serpentine sideboard, a chinoiserie corner cupboard and a second grandfather clock among other things; all beautiful, all 18th century.

Everything is relative, as the old lady who came to the door would attest, and this little house, with its open fire and unheated shower room, is luxury accommodation when compared with Guy's previous, more temporary domestic arrangements. 'I bought it in my early forties, 12 years ago. Before that, from my late teens when I was expelled from boarding school and lived on the road for a few years, I spent time in some much smaller spaces and some much colder ones,' he says. An early example was the dilapidated pigsty he would 'creep along the hedge and dive into for the night', but there was also a stint squatting in 'an old shepherd's hut in the middle of nowhere', and a summer living in a Morris ambulance. More recently, he occupied the top floor of the servants' wing in a Victorian stately home. 'The rooms were a good size, but the fireplaces were minute. It was arctic.'

This is the first house Guy has owned, and he brought a few pieces of furniture with him, including the 1705 chinoiserie clock in the living room, and the 1800 four-poster bed that he found in pieces in a barn.

LEFT AND ABOVE All that remains of the fitted kitchen that was here when Guy bought the house is the stainless-steel sink under the window, which he is planning to swap for an old Belfast sink with a wooden drainer. He cooks on an old Baby Belling given to him by a friend. This and the electric toaster are his only electrical appliances, and both are discreetly hidden behind a damask-covered screen. The door into the shower room can be seen on the right.

LEFT AND ABOVE All that remains of the fitted kitchen that was here when Guy bought the house is the stainless-steel sink under the window, which he is planning to swap for an old Belfast sink with a wooden drainer. He cooks on an old Baby Belling given to him by a friend. This and the electric toaster are his only electrical appliances, and both are discreetly hidden behind a damask-covered screen. The door into the shower room can be seen on the right.

OPPOSITE The view through the open front door is straight into the so-called kitchen, a room that is furnished more like a rather crowded rectory dining room. Guy's collection of vintage jackets hangs to the left of the door at the bottom of the stairs. The exceptional quality of his furnishings is largely due to his eagle eye and abilities as a furniture restorer. 'I never have any money, so I have to find and mend things, or barter.'

'Aside from being affordable, I had to find a house with enough height for the clock and space for the bed.' The clock brushes the ceiling, and the bed is a very tight squeeze, requiring a neat back flip across the mattress to reach the window on the far side.

Guy has collected antiques since childhood, inspired by the chilly rooms of his prep school in a stately home that had kept some of its furnishings. But his taste has become increasingly refined, and his knowledge honed by years of hands-on experience as a restorer for those local dealers who specialize in Georgian furniture. 'I find some really good pieces on eBay,' he says, 'though I prefer to see and examine furniture, as it's hard to judge patina from a photograph.' He recently spotted a small dressing stand on the Instagram account of a dealer he knows well, who let him take it for restoration, and defer payment. 'It's in pretty bad condition, but the dealer now thinks it might be Chippendale,' says Guy. 'I will have to sell something to find a space for it.'

OPPOSITE The extension is single-storey and upstairs there are just two rooms, this front bedroom and a box bedroom, which Guy uses as a walk-in cupboard. He already owned the 18th-century four-poster bed, which he found in pieces, covered in sheep muck and tied up with baler twine in a barn. He restored it, using antique velvet curtains for its hangings, and when house-hunting had to be sure that it would fit. As it is, it almost fills the room such that Guy has to vault across it to get from one side to the other, or edge round the side.

ABOVE The tiny landing is lit by a window at the top of the stairs, and the doorway to the box room is hung with a pair of antique curtains that take up less space than a door.

ABOVE RIGHT AND RIGHT Guy made the patchwork quilt himself, hand sewing it from scraps of antique textiles. Despite the space taken up by the bed, he has still managed to squeeze into the room a corner cupboard, tripod table, side table and chest of drawers, plus a tight hang of pictures and mirrors and his favourite clock.

ARTS AND LETTERS

Climb the four flights of stairs to Simon Martin's flat in Brighton, step into his tiny book-lined hall, turn left at the shoe rack and you can be in little doubt that this is the home of an art lover. Ascending the last steep hairpin that leads to the top of this tall, terraced Regency house, the walls are tessellated with pictures, at first a mosaic of monochrome etchings and engravings, then as you reach the landing blossoming into the muted colour of drawings, linocuts and paintings. 'That's an Edward Burra etching, those are both Edward Bawden, that's St James' Park by Julian Trevelyan,' and then, as we reach the top, 'another Bawden, a linocut by Enid Marx...oh, and a landscape by Barnett Freedman.'

ALL OF WHICH SHOULD BE AMPLE PREPARATION for the sight through the open door to the front living room of what looks like an oversized folding chair, textured and dripping with a thick blanket of paint in pink, yellow and red – a piece by Phyllida Barlow that Simon was prescient enough to pick up for just £70 in 2007. 'I decided to push myself and buy something out of my comfort zone. It was in storage for years – this flat is extremely small and what you see here in terms of pictures and books is just the tip of an iceberg. But I haven't regretted retrieving this piece – it more than deserves the space.'

ABOVE LEFT AND LEFT The stairs that lead from Simon's front door to his flat are lined with prints and engravings by a selection of artists including Edward Burra, Ian Hamilton Finlay and Edward Bawden, all with white mounts and black frames. The lowered blind in a Sarah Burns fabric helps prevent fading. The plaster sculpture on the window sill is *Echo and Narcissus* by Glyn Philpot.

OPPOSITE The landing provides storage space for stacked copies of *The World of Interiors* beneath a cabinet of curiosities holding things as diverse as a souvenir head of Michelangelo's *David* brought back from Simon's first trip to Italy aged 16 to a sculpture by Paolozzi. The cupboard behind the chair holds the washing machine, vacuum cleaner, ironing board and a clothes rail of jackets.

Small it may be – one room at the front with a spur of wall separating the galley kitchen, a bedroom at the back and a bathroom in between the two, plus a paving-stone-sized square of entrance hall and a strip of landing – but the flat has an advantage Simon has found impossible to replicate. The curve of bay window has a view of the sea to the right and the communal garden ahead, while the left-hand panes are filled by the canopy of a lime tree. 'In summer I nip down to the beach and swim twice a day,' he says. Both view and location are hard to beat, and so it is that unseen pictures accumulate, and an overspill of books forms a wall two deep behind the chaise longue.

Simon is director of the Pallant House Gallery in Chichester, a post he has held since 2017. He has curated a number of high-profile

exhibitions, and written catalogues, monographs and books on artists Glyn Philpot, Eduardo Paolozzi and John Piper, among others. As he talks about the art on his walls, it becomes apparent that much of it is by friends. The same is true of the studio pottery, some of which is arranged on the shelves of the fitted dresser/hutch. 'The yellow tea bowl is by Emmanuel Cooper and was a house-warming present from him, and the cup next to it is by Shozo Michikawa – I stayed with him when I was International Art Advisor to a museum. The jug is by Ursula Mommens, whom I came to know after interviewing her for her centenary.' Everything is here for a reason and has a meaning or a connection, even the cushion in a fabric by Vanessa Bell – 'I used to be a trustee of Charleston.'

You wonder how he has fitted so much into his 46 years. 'I don't have a television,' he says. But this is someone who, aged eight, raised £25 doing jobs like cleaning the car for 50p in order to buy a longed-for shed to put at the bottom of his parents' garden, a shed that he then furnished and surrounded with a herb garden. 'I wanted to be a garden designer as a teenager,' he says. Instead, partly inspired by Sister Wendy's *Story of Painting* television show, he did an extra A-Level at evening classes in order to qualify to study Art History at Warwick, followed by an MA at The Courtauld.

'The art world isn't well-paid,' Simon says. 'I rented in Brighton for ten years until I could afford to buy this in 2012. It was in a horrific state, and had Artex on the ceilings, a 1970s glass screen dividing the kitchen and no fireplace.' He found a chimneypiece on eBay from a house on the seafront,

LEFT In the living room, books have spilled out of the bookcases to form piles two deep behind the chaise longue. Simon says this is just the tip of the iceberg and that he has many more books and pictures in storage. The front cushion on the chaise longue is in a design by Vanessa Bell – Simon was a trustee of her home Charleston for six years.

OPPOSITE AND BELOW The living room had lost its chimneypiece, but Simon found one reclaimed from a house on the seafront. Above it hangs an engraving by Richard Bawden, Edward Bawden's son, entitled *The Cardew Bowl*, and the lower two linocuts on either side are by Simon's friend, artist Christopher Brown. Chairs are upholstered in Zig Zag by Enid Marx and the pots on the antique gramophone are by Phil Rogers. Simon bought the plaster figure of a seated man from a local antiques shop and thinks it is probably by Glyn Philpot.

RIGHT The figures and furniture grouped on top of the small bookcase are ceramics by Katharine Morling.

THIS PAGE Colourful tins are stacked in a corner of the kitchen counter, plates and mugs are stored on a plate rack. This space also has its complement of art, including a watercolour still life over the sink by Laurence Wallace. Next to it is a hand-printed silver gelatine photograph by Rachel Whiteread.

OPPOSITE A round Ercol table sits nicely in the curve of the bay in front of the fitted dresser/hutch, which holds plates by Eric Ravilious, antique Staffordshire flatback figures and studio pottery by Phil Rogers, Richard Batterham and Emmanuel Cooper, among others. The chairs came from a cafe on the seafront.

walls and ceilings were replastered and the glass partition replaced by matchboarding salvaged from a shop. This and the matchboarding in the kitchen, the dresser/hutch shelves and the window frames have all recently been painted black, and last year the pale grey walls were given a coat of imperial yellow. He is pleased by how well these strong colours work as a background for his collections.

As well as art, studio pottery and Staffordshire figures, Simon has an extensive collection of bookplates, many designed by well-known artists for well-known book lovers. Luckily these can be kept in boxes under the bed.

LEFT AND OPPOSITE The bedroom at the back of the flat contains more bookcases and pictures propped on the floor as well as hung on the walls. The geese on the curtains in a design from 1938 by EQ Nicholson are echoed in a coathanger on the cupboard handle by Icelandic designer Ingibjörg Hanna Bjarnadottir. A tailor's dummy is dressed in a jewel-bright kimono made for Simon by his friend Sarah Arnett. Above the brass bedstead is a painting by Louise Bristow and propped next to it is a portrait of Simon by Peter James Field.

ABOVE The bathroom is sandwiched between the living room and the bedroom and has a wall of postcards of favourite paintings and images spanning the history of art, from classical Rome to the 20th century.

LUDLOW LOVE

Libby Lord hasn't always been a decorator, but all the signs were there. One of three children brought up in a Staffordshire mining cottage, she chose to paint the bedroom she shared with her sister in sunshine yellow, including the wardrobe and chest of drawers. Her grandpa owned an ironmonger's shop that sold paint. 'He put up a new Sanderson wallpaper in his 1970s bungalow every two years,' she says, 'and I loved that.' Most telling of all, she wasn't satisfied with her Barbie house. 'I extended it with cardboard boxes and decorated the rooms with scraps from my mum's sewing box. It was the envy of my friends.'

LIBBY WANTED TO BE AN ACTRESS, studied art and drama and then trained as a teacher, but she always painted and made things, and managed to spend her twenties earning a living as an artist, selling prints and greetings cards and designing packaging. In 1999 she moved to Ludlow and had a studio above the renowned Ludlow Period House Shop. This turned into a job running their Shrewsbury shop, from where she was headhunted by an interior decorator who taught her that 'curtains were not boring', among other things. In 2018 she set up on her own. 'It was a bit of a long road,' Libby says, 'but I am now doing what I most love.'

Her terraced Regency cottage is a glorious testament to that love. 'It's not a lot of space to play with,' she admits, 'but I have decorated the hell out of what there is.' She and her partner Ed Sinclair, who runs the Harp Lane Deli in the centre of the town, bought the house in 2017. 'It was very 1970s, and very damp, but the previous owner had knocked the two downstairs rooms into one, which we liked.

ABOVE LEFT AND LEFT The house is one of a terrace built by a Whig politician at the beginning of the 19th century as a bribe to potential supporters who had to be property owners in order to vote. Libby has crammed the small garden with all her favourite flowering plants.

OPPOSITE Shelving above the kitchen windows is hung from Scandinavian 'string' brackets because there is no space to attach standard shelf brackets, and houses Ed's extensive collection of cookery books. Below are blinds in Pavilion Stripe from Bennison Fabrics.

BELOW Libby bought the glass-fronted wall cabinet from her friend Guy Marshall (see pages 24–37) and uses it to display her Barker Bros Nasturtium crockery, here seen next to the real thing picked from the garden. The column pepper mill is from Berdoulat.

RIGHT The rear wall of the kitchen was once the outside wall of the back of the house, and the door and window aperture remain. The window now serves as a hatch linking the kitchen with the table on its far side. The wallpaper from the other side of the kitchen wall has been used to paper the embrasure.

We had to strip off the gypsum plaster and replace it with lime, put in a new kitchen and bathroom and excavate to find the original living-room fireplace. When we first lit the new wood burner, there was a strong smell of bread from the warmed-up old bricks – a memory of the people who once lived and cooked here before the kitchen extension was built.'

The house is built over three floors, each one with two rooms, plus a tiny bathroom on the first floor and an even tinier shower room hidden in a cupboard on the top floor. 'A lot of people choose to make a first-floor room into a sitting room,' says Libby, 'but we wanted space for Ed's three children to stay, so have kept the upstairs as bedrooms. The ground-floor room has to function as living room, dining room and study.

OPPOSITE The ground floor was originally two rooms. The large alcove opposite the table encloses a wall of reclaimed floor-to-ceiling cupboard doors hiding a second refrigerator and freezer, the washing machine, the vacuum cleaner and 'all the other things you don't want to be seen'. A curtain in Flora Soames Dahlias screens one end of this 'pantry' area.

BELOW The alcove on the right of the fireplace features a large drip-pattern footed bowl from Puglia between a pair of 18th-century newel posts from Marc Kitchen-Smith.

RIGHT The dresser/hutch came from Libby's friend Tim Smith (see pages 140–153) and is loaded with eBay and flea-market finds. Libby says they tried no less than five different dining tables before they found this one, which is unusually narrow but can seat eight when pulled out. It is a collapsible Welsh village hall table from Baileys Home in Ross-on-Wye. A 19th-century French textile design is pinned up next to the pheasant chargers on the dresser/hutch, while the lichen-like Squiggle wallpaper from Colefax and Fowler on the end wall helps to bring the garden indoors.

LEFT Libby installed the wood burner and when it was first lit there was a distinct smell of baking bread, an olfactory memory from when this fireplace was used for cooking. On either side, the twin chairs are upholstered in Meander by Josef and Anni Albers from Christopher Farr, now discontinued. The television is in the niche on the left of the fireplace on a lever bracket, hidden behind a panel of Jemma Lewis's marbled paper when not in use.

I have decorated several of the many large, grand townhouses in Ludlow, but there is something wonderful about being let loose on a small one. You can make mistakes and it's not too expensive to put them right – and you can have a lot of what you fancy, just in small helpings.'

It's a formula that has resulted in a decorative tasting menu of delights. Behind the bright green front door and pots of red geraniums and velvety black petunias on the narrow front steps, a staircase of stripes rises up between walls garlanded with flowers, leaves and coiling tendrils, in a facsimile of a design taken from an 18th-century screen. The front door has an inner curtain of striped floral brocade, and the door on the left opens into the living room, which Libby describes as 'a cottage pattern cacophony'. Certainly nothing matches and it is true that there are more different designs than you can shake a stick at: curtains splashed with multicoloured foxgloves, cushions sprinkled with violas, fat stripes, thin stripes, chairs in a geometric print, a zigzag of tiling in the hearth, marbled lampshades

PAGES 58–59 Having been promised that the sofa from Dudgeon would definitely fit through the door, after four different attempts it was eventually delivered in pieces and reassembled and upholstered on site. Cushions are in Tazuna by Robert Kime and Squiggle by Colefax and Fowler, with the smallest in Plain Stripe from Bennison. The foxglove window curtains are Lustmore from Jean Monro and the front door curtain in the background is in Moire Montrachet from Charles Burger, which Libby found on eBay.

TOP AND ABOVE The first two flights of stairs in the house are papered in what Libby says is 'the most wonderful wallpaper I have ever seen', Le Paravent Chinois by John Derian for Pierre Frey. She is saving up to take it all the way to the top floor. The lamp on the antique stool is an original 1970s Tizio by Richard Sapper for Artemide.

LEFT There are two bedrooms and a bathroom on the first floor. This smaller bedroom at the back is used as a dressing room and has a Regency sofa upholstered in Jean Monro's hand-block Rose & Fern facing a 1930s painted wardrobe that Libby bought from an antique dealer in Puglia.

OPPOSITE LEFT In the front bedroom on the third floor, an Ortiz tuna can from Harp Lane Deli stores Libby's collection of earrings. The stump work panel pinned above the chest of drawers came from textile dealer Susy Stirrup and the blind is in a Colefax antique glazed chintz. Door and window surrounds are painted in Ice House Blue from Francesca's Paints.

OPPOSITE RIGHT The same bedroom has an IKEA wardrobe that Libby has customized with panels of Morris & Co. Emery's Willow wallpaper and paint in flat oil from Atelier Ellis in a shade called Waving & Smiling. The antique block-print cushion on the chair is from Tobias and the Angel.

OPPOSITE BELOW The paintings in this bedroom are by Libby, the blue one 'entirely in outrageously expensive lapis lazuli pigment'. Textiles pinned up behind the bed are an 18th-century crewel work fragment, a 19th-century French Indienne border and a 19th-century Italian mezzaro border from antique textiles dealer Katharine Pole.

and a cupboard curtain dense with dahlias. Put together with an eye for colour and balance, the result is informal and charming.

A sofa stretches the whole length of the seating area, and a long narrow table does the same at the dining end of the room. A wall pierced by an unglazed window and door-shaped aperture separates the kitchen and is papered in a grassy green squiggle wallpaper that Libby chose in order to 'bring the garden indoors. I love gardening, so there are flowers everywhere and on everything.'

Libby says the biggest influence on her decorating style has been Ludlow itself. 'A typical townhouse here screams quality, but often has an antiquated kitchen and wonky floorboards. When I am asked to decorate one, the most important thing is not to undo its atmosphere. I prefer cobwebs and scratches to gleaming surfaces, so I am cultivating candle smut and letting the floorboards develop a patina. I like to throw in a curve ball of surprise among the dust, a shocking colour or a dash of the unexpected. But that's very Ludlow too.'

ABOVE AND RIGHT Another wallpaper in an 18th-century design envelopes the front bedroom, this one Swakeley's Chinoiserie from Hamilton Weston, while the festoon blind is in an antique Colefax glazed chintz, as is the frilled bolster. The tallboy holds bed linen and towels and was found on eBay. The painting above the bed is Libby's portrait of their whippet Lady as a puppy.

PAGE 64 AND 65 Libby and Ed's bedroom is on the top floor at the back of the house, overlooking their garden and the gardens of houses in neighbouring streets. Lancaster wallpaper from Jean Monro wraps walls and ceiling, and the striped bedcover was a present to Libby from Ed. Curtains are Ebury from Colefax as are the cushions on the bed in Leaf Damask, chosen to echo the view of next door's fig tree. Behind the wall of matchboarding facing the bed and painted in Coming Up Roses from Atelier Ellis is a tiny bathroom.

FULL HOUSE

At the age of 22, Will Le Clerc arrived at Heathrow with a backpack, a small amount of money and no intention of returning to the 'life of colonial privilege' he had been brought up with on a wealthy farm in South Africa.

'It was cold, wet and miserable. I asked for advice at the information desk, and they suggested a hostel in Piccadilly. I had visited England before with my parents and had formed an irrational, emotional connection with its history, gardens, houses, literature. Despite having no contacts, or even the right clothes, it felt like coming home. I met nice people and within weeks had found a job and a flat.'

TWENTY YEARS ON and Will works in an executive role at Liberty. 'I love the decorative arts, so it's a cruel irony that I have no artistic talent.' He means this in the sense that he cannot draw a horse, but once inside his home in a pretty Kent village it is apparent that what he can do is hunt down beautiful things and arrange them superbly.

Built in the late 19th century as one of three terraced gardeners' cottages for an adjacent estate, the exterior is pretty and adorned with roses yet otherwise unremarkable, with just enough width to park a car. But edge round the vintage Mercedes to the front door, take a single step to the right past the staircase into the front room and you are instantly immersed in a quality of furnishings more

OPPOSITE The living room has contents of a grandeur that is all the more striking for their diminutive setting. The portrait of Sir John Egerton is by Mary Beale and once hung in Heaton Hall. Will claims to have no artistic talent but did a convincing 'weekend DIY job' marbling the wooden chimneypiece.

ABOVE RIGHT The cottage is the middle one of three and is flanked at the back by the gabled extensions of its larger neighbours. The kitchen is single-storey and the long, narrow garden slopes up from its window.

RIGHT The door from the living room into the tiny entrance hall has been beautifully painted on both sides and possibly dates from when the cottages were first built. All the curtains are second-hand; these are Honeysuckle by Colefax and Fowler.

stately home than tiny terrace – antique oil paintings, leather-bound books, sculptures, pottery, porcelain, engravings and intaglios. There is a piano, its lid open as though it has just been played, there are Colefax and Fowler Honeysuckle curtains, a Howard sofa and armchair, a caned armchair and a carpet-covered chest, all slotted into a space in which it would be impossible to swing anything bigger than a hamster. If interior decorating is an art, then Will Le Clerc is an artist.

Through a curtained door from the front room is another room, bigger by the width of the staircase. This is the dining room, complete with 17th-century table, six 18th-century dining chairs, a bust on a marble column, a 17th-century wall tapestry,

PAGES 68–69 Will has managed to fit a grandfather clock into the small square of entrance hall, and a piano, an Edwardian Howard sofa and armchair and a caned armchair into the living room. The portrait over the piano and the one to the right of the doorway are both by 18th-century painter Arthur Devis, one of Will's favourite artists, and the terracotta figurines on the shelf above the door are 19th-century Neapolitan, made as Grand Tour souvenirs and probably by Chiurazzi.

LEFT The living-room window looks out across the main street of the village. Will has found space for a trio of 18th-century portraits hung between the casements.

ABOVE A curtain across the doorway between the living room and dining room saves some wall space for hanging pictures, plates and framed intaglios.

OPPOSITE A handsome 18th-century oak chest on stand faces the fireplace in the dining room where a bronze statue on a marble plinth, bought by Will at auction and much larger and heavier than he imagined when he bid for it, sits in the middle of the dining table.

LEFT Squeezed between the living room and the kitchen, the dining room has antique furnishings of a quality more often seen in a large country house. Vintage Colefax and Fowler curtains hang beneath a pelmet made by Oliver Messel for his house at Pelham Place, and the tapestry is late 16th century.

ABOVE The thickness of what was originally an outer wall allows space for hanging pictures in the opening between the dining room and the kitchen. A door on the right leads into the garden, which is planted with Will's favourite old-fashioned roses, including Madame Hardy and Paul's Himalayan Musk.

Delft plates, a Rococo gilt mirror and another pair of Colefax curtains topped by a painted pelmet. 'The pelmet is by Oliver Messel,' says Will. 'Along with all the iconic English country house furnishings I love so much, I also look out for "outsider art". I have a painting by Rex Whistler, and the portrait over the living room fireplace is by Mary Beale, who, being a woman, has only recently been fully recognized.' Between the dining-room window and another grandfather clock is an opening into the single-storey extension that houses the kitchen with its fitted cupboards painted deep sky blue and a table just big enough for two cereal bowls and a toast rack.

Upstairs are the bathroom and two bedrooms: one with a single four-poster bed hung with floral chintz, the other with a half-tester large enough to stretch across the width of the room from the open door to the cupboards on the far side.

The contents of the house have been accruing for ten years, ever since Will moved here from a larger house he shared with his husband, the celebrated French-Algerian author and poet Xavier Le Clerc. 'Xavier needed to spend more time in France for his work, so we swapped that house for this and a flat in Paris. It was one of the smaller houses I looked at but I fell for it, partly because the previous owner hadn't changed anything, so it had all its original doors, floorboards and fireplaces, and partly because when I viewed I ended up staying and bonding over a mutual love of old English roses. A lot of our furniture was too big – the hardest thing to let go of was my 17th-century bed, which wouldn't fit up the stairs.'

Will confesses that he is 'an obsessive collector – it's more like an addiction. I wake very early for Maya [their 15-year-old spaniel] and spend the time before I get up for work trawling through auction catalogues looking for the things I most love,

PAGE 74 Will decided not to change the cupboards in the kitchen but painted them in Farrow & Ball Cook's Blue. He also managed to find a table for two small enough to fit in the middle.

PAGE 75 The kitchen wallpaper is Mill Oak by Fanny Shorter, and to the left of the door is a dog flap for the couple's spaniels, Maya and Teddy.

ABOVE LEFT A Roger Oates runner carpets the stairs, which are lined with pictures hung on pinned-up pieces of an antique tapestry weave fabric, 'which is the closest I can get to the picture hang at Hatfield House', says Will.

LEFT AND OPPOSITE The guest bedroom is at the front and papered all over and across the ceiling with Colefax and Fowler Seraphina. A small bureau desk sits in the alcove with books heaped on a single shelf above it, many on the subject of English interiors. The armchair is William Morris and the single four-poster bed dates from the early 19th century and is by Heals – 'their golden age', according to Will. The curtains are vintage Colefax and Fowler and match the bed hangings.

which tend to be from the mid-18th century and earlier, whether paintings by Arthur Devis, Grand Tour terracottas or something very specific like a late 17th-century high-backed cane chair.'

By the time you read this, the work of art that is Will's home will have been completely dismantled. Xavier is now spending more time in England and the couple have bought a larger house on the south coast. Early morning trawling has got even more exciting.

OPPOSITE Looking across from the guest bedroom on the first floor there is a view into the bathroom, which has a space-saving shower rather than a tub.

ABOVE The quilt on the guest bed is antique and the bed hangings are vintage Colefax and Fowler.

ABOVE RIGHT A view from the landing down the stairs, where paintings and prints are hung frame to frame. Every available space is used to hang pictures, including the backs of doors and narrow slivers of wall.

RIGHT The bathroom has vintage fittings and matchboard panelling painted in Brinjal by Farrow & Ball with Richmond Park wallpaper by Zoffany on the wall above.

PAGES 80 AND 81 The main bedroom at the back has Willow Boughs wallpaper by William Morris. There was not enough space for Will's 17th-century bedstead, so instead there is a Victorian half-tester. Curtains are vintage Sanderson and the pastel portrait over the chest of drawers is the Marchioness of Downshire by William Hoare.

LITTLE GEM

It's impossible to arrive at Caroline Holdaway and Fatimah Namdar's Cotswold cottage and not exhale a sigh of delight – the sort of sound that comes unbidden at the sight of a chuckling baby or a queue of fluffy yellow ducklings. The steep, stone-tiled roof has a cheeky tilt towards the chimney and the single upstairs window wears a high-gabled hat, with offset beneath it a front door and another small window. The combination of crookedness and asymmetry combined with diminutive size gives the frontage a fairy-tale charm. Better still, the cottage sits on its own, raised up and in front of the cottages next door, its neat, rose-garlanded rectangle of garden laid out before it, 'as if it were a jewel being presented to you on a cushion', says Caroline.

PRETTY THOUGH IT IS, this tiny hamlet sequestered down a series of leafy lanes seems an unlikely home for such an urbane couple, one a successful actress turned successful decorator, the other a renowned portrait photographer. 'We are lucky enough also to have a terraced Victorian house in Highgate,' says Caroline, 'but London is for work, the hairdresser and the dentist. When we talk about "going home", we mean coming here. It's not a weekend cottage – we come for weeks at a time, and as often as we can, winter and summer. We have friends here, the dogs are happy.'

OPPOSITE The front door, on the left, opens straight into the living room. When the house was built 300 years ago, this was the only downstairs room, with a spiral staircase in the corner on the right of the chimney breast. It is now a comfortable living room, with the dining room, kitchen and cloakroom in a late 20th-century extension at the back.

ABOVE RIGHT AND RIGHT The house is a typical Cotswold cottage, built in honey-coloured stone and with a roof of rustic stone tiling with a steep window gable in the middle. Through the front door, framed by pink roses, you see through to the back window of the living room, which now faces the wall of the kitchen extension.

THIS PAGE A deep cushioned sofa faces the fire in the living room and an antique wing chair and footstool have been rejuvenated with upholstery in lilac velvet. Photographs by Fatimah of their dogs and one of Caroline are propped on an elm shelf behind the sofa.

Surprisingly, it was not love at first sight. 'I was doing a big decorating project nearby,' says Caroline, 'one that was a matter of years not months, and we started looking at properties we could afford in the area. We came to see this from the outside, cantered up the drive with excitement, saw the 1990s extension at the back dug into the slope and thought "no". The garden had motorway planting and no enclosing wall, and it all looked rather bare. But we didn't find anything else, so came to view again, and as soon as I stepped through the door into the front room, I changed my mind.'

The original house is nearly 300 years old. Once upon a time – and not so long ago – the sitting room Caroline stepped into was the only downstairs room and had a spiral staircase in a corner to the right of the big stone fireplace.

OPPOSITE Lenny the elderly lurcher sleeps peacefully in the living room next to the doorway into the dining room. Everything beyond this threshold dates from the 1990s, when the cottage was extended. Caroline laid new flooring throughout in reclaimed pitch pine rescued from an old factory, which she found at a reclamation yard. These boards create a flow between rooms that helps to unify the old with the new.

ABOVE The table is laid with some of the green-glazed Biot pottery Caroline and Fatimah have collected over the years in France. Caroline wanted the interior to have the clarity and freshness of a bowl of lemons and limes.

LEFT A large mirror and a double-height ceiling at one end of the dining room bring the interior added light and a feeling of spaciousness. The elm shelving adds an element of the handmade to the 1990s interior architecture and here supports a selection of studio pottery including a huge platter by Clive Bowen.

LEFT Looking back from the kitchen through the dining room to the living room you can see how, as with the flooring, a single paint colour used on walls and woodwork helps to make the original cottage and its recent extension feel as one. The colour is Paint and Paper Library Stone II.

BELOW LEFT Next to the kitchen at the back of the house is a downstairs loo with more elm shelving and another dog portrait by Fatimah. In summer, when the garden is in full bloom, there are roses in every room.

BELOW The original spiral staircase from the living room has long since gone, and a new staircase now rises from the dining room with space next to it for coats and boots. When walking the dogs, the couple use a door into the dining room from the drive at the side of the house rather than the front door.

OPPOSITE The elm shelving supported on simple brackets is a feature of every room in the house, almost a leitmotif, and was made by a retired colleague of Caroline's, who also made the wooden planked doors. Here in the kitchen, the shelves hold green pottery plates that are used every day.

'A previous occupant brought up five children here when it was still only three rooms,' says Fatimah. The 1990s extension is vital extra space and proved more attractive than anticipated; a double-height dining room open to the landing and half the width of the facade that leads to a kitchen and downstairs lavatory, and a second bedroom above. 'We didn't make any structural changes,' says Caroline, 'though we did get planning permission to take out the low ceiling of the front bedroom and extend it into the roof space, which makes the room feel twice the size.'

No knocking down of walls or reordering of space, but they did replace the flooring, none of which was old. 'I always start with floors,' says Caroline. 'What is under your feet is vital to the character and feel of a room. We used pitch pine boards reclaimed from a factory. They still had the memory of painted walkways and machine positions visible, so we laid them out on trestles in the garden and cleaned them with Velcro pads, which is gentle enough to preserve the surface. Once laid it was given a watered-down coat of emulsion and then sealed.' They also put in stone window sills, and doors and shelves made from reclaimed elm. 'We used old-fashioned rose-headed nails – details are so important. The rugs are Scandinavian Kasthall flatweaves, tightly woven from such high-quality wool they last forever.'

LEFT Small as it is, the kitchen extends into an alcove just the right size for an oil-fired Heritage range cooker, leaving space in front of it for Caroline's favourite antique rush-seated chair, made of elm like the shelving. 'It's strong and light and has been crafted with such slender rails – just beautiful,' she says. 'It's where I come to sit in the middle of the night if I can't sleep.'

RIGHT Everything fits neatly, including the pine table under the window. Like all the best kitchens, the room is a perfect mix of the practical and the pleasing, with more studio pottery gathered on the window sill.

Caroline has a great turn of phrase when describing how she decorates. 'I wanted this house to feel like a bowl of lemons and limes – fresh, with a clean, clear palette.' Walls and woodwork are all painted the same shade of off-white, 'one breath of air running throughout'. Craftsmanship is apparent everywhere, from the plain pendant lampshades upstairs hand-trimmed with velvet ribbon, to the studio pottery they collect. 'We both love the colour green,' says Caroline, 'and have been buying Biot greenware over many years of visits to the South of France.' It is obvious the two share an aesthetic. 'We love the same things,' says Caroline, 'but when it comes to decorating, I do the donkey work and Fatimah is invited to clap her hands!' It may be on a small scale, but the design of this cottage undoubtedly deserves a standing ovation.

ABOVE LEFT The stairs are carpeted in a bespoke Kasthall Scandinavian flatweave from Sinclair Till, in a traditional design called Goose Eye. All the rugs in the house are these flatweaves, which Caroline says last forever. 'The rug in the living room is 40 years old and looks as good as new.'

LEFT Another Goose Eye flat weave runs along the landing between Fatimah's bedroom at the back of the house and Caroline's bedroom and the bathroom at the front. The cloth on the table is from Raoul Textiles, whose fabrics Caroline has used in almost every room.

THIS PAGE The elm shelf along the back of the wall in Fatimah's bedroom holds four antique hand-coloured engravings of birds. They are German and were a present to her from Caroline's mother. The lampshade has a trim of velvet ribbon from VV Rouleaux, ribbon that Caroline has also used as appliquéd stripes on the heavy linen door curtain in the living room.

ABOVE LEFT When Caroline and Fatimah first bought the cottage, this bedroom in the original part of the house had a particularly low ceiling, which planning officers thought should stay as part of the old fabric of the house. Fortunately, Caroline found traces of distemper on one of the beams, proving that raising the ceiling into the pitch of the roof was not a new idea.

ABOVE One of the interior architectural changes Caroline made was to replace the later wooden window sills with stone, 'for texture and character'. She also added folding shutters, which she has used throughout instead of curtains.

LEFT The bathroom has been panelled with reclaimed matchboarding. Here again are elm shelves, providing useful storage as well as somewhere to put a vase of garden flowers.

OPPOSITE Caroline's bed is against the chimney flue from the living-room fireplace, and she has used its shelf to display three pieces of antique lustreware. Green is Caroline's favourite colour, and the green of her linen bedspread reflects the view through her window of trees and fields.

GOOD MOVES

In a corner of Russell Loughlan's poised, colour-drenched living room, there is a table with an arrangement of things on it: a lamp with a carved alabaster base and tall pleated shade, a small slipware plate, a barley twist candlestick and a slightly naive carving of a girl with her hands raised to her head.

I T'S ONE OF MANY PLEASING GROUPINGS, whether the drip-glaze pots on shelves, or the vintage plates hung horizontally and off-centre on a slice of wall that marks where the front-to-back space was once two separate rooms. 'We found that lamp base buried in rubble when we tanked the basement,' says Russell. 'I got the shade and slipware dish in a charity shop, the candlestick was from the market, the sculpture cost £15 from a shop down the road, and I found the table on the street.'

Russell is good at spotting a bargain, and at seeing beauty in things that others might disregard. In the same room, the standout piece of art is a framed antique Japanese embroidery on silk with flowers, leaves and birds, their elegance and delicacy in sharp contrast to the battered panels they are mounted on. 'Those are the only two surviving bits of a four-panel screen I got from my mum who had an antiques and junk shop in Leicester where I was born. I carried it around for 30 years as it got more and more dilapidated,' says Russell. 'Most people would have thrown it away, but when I moved here a couple of years ago I had it framed, and it was the starting point for the colour scheme in this room.'

ABOVE LEFT The ground floor was originally divided into two rooms, one at the front and one at the back, with a narrow staircase hall. Sections of supporting wall remain, but the rest have been removed to create a single open-plan space.

LEFT Russell gave the old floorboards a deep clean and a high polish. He also painted the stripes on the walls.

OPPOSITE The colours in this room have a distinctly Pompeian feel and are all in Farrow & Ball Dead Flat paints, the walls in Cat's Paw, the yellow woodwork, shutters and radiator in Cane and the vestibule and stairs in Etruscan Red. Two panels of embroidery from a Japanese screen that Russell had framed and which now hang on the wall behind the sofa were the starting point for the colour scheme.

PAGES 98–99 Many of the period features from this early 18th-century house had been lost, but Russell found a pair of shutters on eBay rescued from a florist in France that exactly fitted the front window and painted a frame around the fireplace in lieu of a chimneypiece. He found the pair of antique French carpet chairs with their crocheted patches in a local shop, Will & Yates.

LEFT The fireplace at the dining end of the room has been tiled with antique manganese Delft tiles collected over a number of years. To its left is Russell's 'thrift corner' – all pieces found in charity shops, junk shops or on the street. The alabaster lamp base was unearthed in the basement when renovating.

OPPOSITE A door under the stairs opens onto a second staircase down to the basement. The table and chapel chairs all came from Will & Yates, and the Japanese watercolour on silk was found in a local junk shop.

He is also good at doing up houses. 'I studied fashion and textiles at St Martins,' he says, 'but I always wanted to be an interior designer.' Having worked in fashion and beauty PR and freelanced as an artist and illustrator while at the same time renovating a series of houses in London and then Deal, Russell has at last established himself as a decorator and is working on several projects including a house in Dalston, London and the interior of a yacht in Nova Scotia. 'All my work has come through word of mouth and Instagram,' he says.

This Georgian terraced house on a residential street five minutes from the seafront is his fifth in Deal. 'The first was a second home escape from London for weekends and holidays. My partner at the time was born in Ramsgate. We explored all the towns along this

coast and decided Deal was our favourite – it hasn't been spoilt and it's a hub for arty, theatrical people. When we came to view potential houses, we met two other couples in the pub and realized we were all interested in the same three properties. We each got the one we wanted, and we've stayed friends. Since Covid, Deal has become my first and only home and I like it that way. It feels like being on holiday every day.'

In comparison with previous restoration projects – Russell bought his last house at auction only to discover it was riddled with rot – this one has proved relatively straightforward. 'It's smaller but feels spacious because the downstairs rooms have been knocked into one.' The entrance hall is a glazed cubicle, so this double room spans the width and depth of the house. A single-storey kitchen extension stretches into the garden, and upstairs are two bedrooms and a bathroom, the front bedroom with a ceiling that now slopes up into the pitch of the roof – another effective space-expanding alteration.

ABOVE The narrow kitchen extends out into the garden with a cloakroom at its far end. Russell found the panel of vintage stained glass on eBay and it almost exactly fitted the old window aperture between the two rooms.

RIGHT Walls in the kitchen and cloakroom are decorated with antique and vintage plates found in local charity shops. The work surfaces are African marble, and the glass light fitting was bought from Etsy and refurbished by a local company.

OPPOSITE The woodwork in the kitchen is Farrow & Ball Green Smoke and the walls are Old White. Moroccan zellige tiles from the Mosaic Factory run along the wall behind the cooker and the spotlights are from Corston. The fitted corner cupboard is original. Russell added the holes for extra ventilation.

PAGES 104 AND 105 Russell says the bathroom was inspired by his 'love affair with Portugal'. He found the mirrors in Lisbon and the antique pulled-thread tablecloth, which he has used as a curtain, at a flea market in Porto. The wall tiles are Mexican from Milagros London, and the floor is painted in Farrow & Ball Radicchio and Dimity, with woodwork in Serge and a cupboard in Sudbury Yellow.

'I put in French doors, tongue-and-groove panelling, a new kitchen and bathroom and new sash windows. But all the fireplaces and floorboards were here.'

Russell sold his previous house with much of its contents – 'the buyers wanted the "look"'– so has found furnishings specifically to suit his new home, whether sourced locally or online. But the most striking aspect of these few rooms is colour – punchy downstairs, with a smart school uniform combination of mustard yellow and terracotta, and so confidently contrapuntal upstairs that looking from the bathroom across the landing to the front bedroom you get an eyeful of every primary and a few secondaries

THIS PAGE AND OPPOSITE A door in Farrow & Ball bright green Raw Tomatillo opens from the landing into the guest bedroom, with its mix of ice-cream colours and stripy walls, hand-painted by Russell in three different shades of Farrow & Ball pink: Templeton Pink, Setting Plaster, and Pink Ground. The IKEA four-poster bed, upcycled and painted, is covered in a plum-coloured Welsh blanket from Will & Yates.

OPPOSITE At the front of the house, its two windows looking out onto the street, is the main bedroom, which feels bigger than its square footage thanks to its ceiling, which rises into the pitch of the roof. The large oil paintings are by local artist Arthur Neal.

too. 'I've never been afraid of it,' says Russell, 'probably helped by my background in fashion and textiles.'

The main bedroom is painted in three different shades of saturated summer-sky blue. On the mantelpiece are two model yachts. 'The one on the right belonged to my ex-partner's dad, but it was broken and had no stand, so I chucked it out on a skip [dumpster] when renovating the last house. A year-and-a-half later, I saw it in a shop down the road, mended and with a stand. It was £55 but I had to buy it.'

ABOVE A BasShu quilt from Will & Yates was the starting point for the colour scheme, with walls in Oval Room Blue, panelled ceiling in Light Blue and woodwork, fireplace and shutters in Sloe Blue, all Farrow & Ball Dead Flat. The model yacht on the right is the one Russell threw away and then bought back.

CONCRETE BENEFITS

'I've always loved Brutalism,' says Tom Morris. 'I was brought up in Portsmouth and we often used to drive past the Tricorn Centre, which was a steel and concrete multiplex built in the '60s, and I think was voted the third ugliest building in Britain in the 1980s. I didn't agree. I was fascinated by its powerful angles and shapes. It was knocked down when I left school, but it stayed with me, and one day I got a bit lost visiting the Barbican, as you do, and started to wonder what it would be like to live in one of the flats here.'

AS BRITAIN'S BEST-KNOWN AMBASSADOR for Brutalism, the Barbican has fared rather better than the Tricorn. Presented with 16 hectares/40 acres of bomb-damaged Central London, architects Chamberlin, Powell and Bon came up with an ambitious scheme of 2000 flats, maisonettes and houses raised above street level and encompassing a church, schools, library, artificial lake, tennis courts and what is still the largest performing arts centre in Europe. Constructed between 1965 and 1982, the whole site was awarded a Grade II listing less than 20 years after completion.

Tom is almost evangelical about its design and community. 'I was lucky enough to be able to buy one of the top-floor flats ten years ago,' he says. 'They are the smallest units but very cleverly arranged.

OPPOSITE The front door of the flat opens into an entrance hall that flows into the living room on its left. Tom upholstered the rectilinear Corbusier chair in a luxurious brown velvet from Rose Uniacke. The early 20th-century table next to it is Liberty & Co.

ABOVE RIGHT Next to the front door is a second door to a large cupboard of three shelves, the bottom one for rubbish sacks, the other two for milk deliveries and post. These are accessed from the landing outside the flat to the left of the front door. Milk is no longer delivered, but rubbish is collected from here and post arrives.

RIGHT The view from the entrance hall to the sliding glass doors of the living room. These open onto a small balcony with a view of cranes and construction sites and the dome of St Paul's Cathedral.

THIS PAGE The room is flooded with light thanks to the glazed sliding door and the semicircular window above. Furniture, including a Søren Lund sofa upholstered in a Kvadrat wool, is arranged on a striped Moroccan flatweave rug from Larusi. The wall colour is Farrow & Ball Salon Drab.

I have a balcony with a view of St Paul's. And at weekends, when there is less traffic, all I can hear is bells, birdsong and the thwack of tennis balls from people playing on the courts below. Far from brutal, it feels safe and peaceful.'

The layout is as simple as it is effective; a flight of stairs leads from the lift/elevator to a landing shared by two flats. Tom's door is to the right and opens into a hallway that flows into the sitting room at the front and to a glazed door and wall at the back, through which you can see into the bedroom. Doors from the hall open into a separate lavatory and bathroom. A galley kitchen behind the wall of the hall has double doors into the sitting room and is lit from a high window where its wall meets the half-dome of its ceiling. The hall is the only space with a lower, flat ceiling and has frosted windows onto the stairwell.

ABOVE AND OPPOSITE The galley kitchen can be separated from the living room by double doors and shares the same high ceiling with a window in it above the right-hand counter. All the units and the electric hob/stovetop are original, made by Brooke Marine who constructed and fitted out boats and small ships. Kitchen walls are painted in Olive Colour from Little Greene, while the four pottery plates hanging above the counter are from Andalusia.

RIGHT A pair of rush-seated chairs designed by William Morris for Liberty & Co stand by the sliding door of the living room and in front of the String shelving unit. The chunky slab pots on the top shelf are pieces made by Tom, who was inspired to take up pottery classes when he wrote a book about contemporary ceramics called *New Wave Clay*.

OPPOSITE AND RIGHT The only major change Tom made to the interior fabric of the flat was to lay hardwood flooring that now runs throughout, aside from in the bathroom, which has tiled flooring, and the bedroom, with its fitted carpet. Tom describes the dining table as 'mid-century generic teak', while the chairs are 1920s bentwood bistro chairs. The coffee table beyond is 1970s smoked glass. Wall-mounted kitchen cupboards have sliding doors also in semi-opaque glass.

ABOVE A line of stripy cushions picks up the wider stripes of the rug. Hanging over the sofa is a traditional Japanese jacket, which has the characters for 'wood' on the back and may have been worn by a tree feller or a carpenter.

PAGE 118 The entrance hall links the living room at the front and the bedroom at the back, with kitchen, bathroom and separate loo in the space between.

ABOVE AND RIGHT The loo has walls in Masai by Paint and Paper Library and a ceiling that glows with Farrow & Ball India Yellow. The Twyfords Barbican basin was specially designed to sit as close against the wall as possible and has just gone back into production. The bathroom has its original fittings and wrap-around plain tiling, warmed up by a contemporary rug from Larusi.

The differing heights and free flow of light from three directions maximize character and create a feeling of openness in defiance of the minimal square footage.

'Even better,' says Tom, 'the flat had all its original fittings.' The loo has a wall-hung basin with integrated soap dish and side-mounted spout that manages only to protrude a matter of inches. The fitted kitchen was made by a firm who supplied yachts and has an almost space-age sleekness. It incorporates a pioneering waste-disposal unit that still works. Household rubbish is collected from a double-sided hatch next to the front door. 'It was also designed for post and milk deliveries, though we all buy milk from the supermarket nowadays.'

While living here, Tom has performed a gentle pivot from a career in design journalism to become a designer himself. In 2018, after a post-graduate diploma in Interior Design, he set up Morrisstudio and only six years later was included in *House & Garden* magazine's list of the top 100 interior designers. They are now a team of three and Tom describes their work as 'craft-based' and 'story-led'. 'I wrote a

book about ceramics, *New Wave Clay*, which was published the same year I founded the studio,' Tom says. 'Our projects always have an emphasis on the handmade.'

The pivot has taken him back to a childhood ambition. 'I was constantly decorating my bedroom at home. It was peak *Changing Rooms*, and I had one wall rag-rolled in lime green and I scumble-glazed all the furniture. But I was at Portsmouth Grammar, which was very naval, and interior decorating wasn't on the radar. The closest I could get was to read History of Art at UCL.'

Tom has given the flat several makeovers. 'When I first moved in, I painted it white and put down flooring in a tropical hardwood. The flooring stayed but I have changed the paint colours so many times I've probably made it significantly smaller.' Furnishings are a mix of classics by William Morris, Le Corbusier and Liberty, and mid-century finds. In pride of place on the String shelving unit are some slab pots he made himself. Just below is a bowl by Bernard Leach. 'I treat myself to a new piece of studio pottery every time I get royalties from my book.'

THIS PAGE Billy bookcases from IKEA surround the window and fill one wall of the entrance hall where a blue roller blind picks up the colour of the Sargadelos ceramics on the window sill. Tom collected the model aeroplanes lined up on the top shelf on his travels as an editor at *Monocle* magazine. Propped beneath the window is an antique tribal sun mask from Burkina Faso bought at Lots Road Auctions.

THIS PAGE AND OPPOSITE A door from the bedroom leads onto a walkway that runs the length of these top-floor flats and looks over the garden square around which they are built. Tom bought the hanging above the bed a few years ago while travelling in Myanmar. 'It's made by the Chin tribespeople in the far north, and there are some rather creepy goings-on in the embroidery.' The headboard is covered in African kente cloth, the bedside tables/nightstands are mid-century Italian and the lamps are Pooky with vintage shades. A group of ceramics on the chest of drawers at the end of the bed includes pieces by Paul Philp and Dylan Bowen. Walls are painted in Farrow & Ball Light Gray.

ROOMS WITH A VIEW

In her early twenties, Victoria Bonham Carter was taken by a friend to visit a row of eight remote coastguard cottages overlooking the Solent. 'I still remember driving down the long gravel track and that first sight of the sea as you turn the corner, and then the cottages lined up along the beach and the Isle of Wight across the water. So many birds – black-headed gulls, oystercatchers, curlews – no traffic, just the sea and sky. It hit me in the solar plexus and I decided I had to find a way to come here as often as possible.'

A FEW DAYS LATER SHE CAME BACK ON HER OWN. 'I knocked on every door and asked if I could borrow a room. To my amazement, Hugh and Margaret Casson's daughter said I could stay in their cottage when they weren't using it. Which is exactly what I did for ten years. Sailing has been a huge part of my life since childhood and there is a sailing club at the end of the track, five minutes from the cottages. It's my idea of heaven. Coming here was so important to me that I was terrified when I first brought Ed in case he didn't "get it".'

Luckily he very much did. The cottages are rented from the Beaulieu Estate, and not long after they married, Victoria and Edward were offered one of their own. Edward learned to sail and in due course so did their three children. 'Even though they are all grown up and doing their own thing, they love coming here as much as ever,' says Victoria. 'I teach sailing all through the summer and run the racing events. Ed is my trusty crew in our scow. I have to be dragged back to our house in London.'

ABOVE LEFT The cottages at either end of the row are larger and were for the use of senior coastguards. The middle window of the bay has been converted to a door that opens into the small back garden, which is separated from the beach by a fence and a grassy bank.

LEFT A bright red front door opens onto a hall with the kitchen off to the left, the bathroom and stairs to the right, and the living room ahead, with its glorious views of the sea through the bay window.

THIS PAGE Fitted bench seating around the table in the living room maximizes seating capacity. The pottery jug holding flowers from the garden was commissioned by Victoria from Harry Juniper as a present for Edward to celebrate their 14th wedding anniversary and features animals associated with their three children. The walls and curtains are sunbleached to the softest shades of pink and blue.

THIS PAGE The open door from the living room frames a perfect living picture of the garden fence and grass in the foreground, the waters of the Solent in the middle ground and the Isle of Wight in the distance. Floors are painted wood. A flatweave rug in the blues of sea and sky marks out the seating area in front of the fireplace.

LEFT The mantelpiece is crowded with postcards, photographs and mementos, including a cut-out of Victoria with a sailing cup and their son Tobias playing the trumpet as a boy. There is also a collection of 'nesting' pebbles found on the beach on display.

RIGHT To the left of the front porch, the original small-paned kitchen window has an unusual sideways opening. Built of brick with slate roofs, the cottages were designed to withstand all weathers in their exposed coastal position.

Built in 1860 for coastguards on the frontline against smugglers, the line of brick cottages stands firm against the wind and waves, plain and sturdy with steeply pitched roofs, the six central ones bookended by two larger ones that boast the extra status of bay windows to befit the senior coastguards they housed. Victoria and Edward's is one of these and its neat little kitchen and adjacent living room have unusually high ceilings. The downstairs bathroom is tucked under the single-storey slope of roof shared by the entrance hall, and at the top of the white-painted curl of steep wooden stairs are three diminutive bedrooms, the two at the front looking out to sea.

Victoria describes the cottage as a 'sail locker' and designed the interior to be practical, with painted wooden floors for sandy feet and an Everhot in the kitchen for drying damp clothing. 'I studied stage and costume design at the Bristol Old Vic Theatre School, and I see interiors like stage sets.'

RIGHT At the centre of the kitchen is an Everhot stove, essential for drying out wet sailing gear. Victoria and Edward have been coming here since before they were married, and inside the door reveal a record of their three children's heights over the years has been preserved and painted around.

THIS PAGE A pair of deep sofas face each other on either side of the fireplace with cushions and throws, many of which are made with antique textiles bought online from Francesca Gentilli. The room is full of images of ships and seabirds, with an embroidery of a curlew on the left of the chimney breast balanced by a cased taxidermy curlew on the right.

THIS PAGE Shelves over the dining table display a collection of antique lustreware and Mocha ware china. The small Festival of Britain mug at bottom right is a 'homage' to Hugh Casson, who generously allowed Victoria to stay in his cottage next door. The painting is by Ramiro Fernandez Saus.

You decorate and furnish the space and then watch the play. This has always been a house for holidays – for freedom, fresh air, all those old-fashioned childhood joys. I think that's why I have never changed the children's room – it still has their three little beds and the cushions with dogs on that belonged to my mother and aunt.'

The living room with its deep sofas and dining table is the centre of family life. 'I wanted the colours to be like a raspberry ripple,' says Victoria. Walls are painted a pink that she says has faded to be even prettier over the years. The sun has had exactly the same effect on the curtains, their pale blue pattern bleached to vanishing at the edges. Cushions and throws in soft pastels are a mix of the vintage and antique fabrics Victoria has always loved and collected. And pictures include works by favourite artists

THIS PAGE Above one of the sofas is another curlew, this one a collage by Kate Black. A collection of sea glass is arranged along the shelf behind the fitted benches and another of pebbles in graded colours, inspired by Kettle's Yard, which is one of Victoria's best-loved interiors. More pebbles, these from Île de Ré where the family have an annual holiday, are lined up on the mantelpiece in front of one of a pair of antique angel candlesticks.

THIS PAGE Looking from the living room back into the hall, the stairs and bathroom are on the left. The oil painting is a portrait of their dog Daisy, painted by Victoria who took art classes with artist Anthea Craigmyle. The prints of ducks above the sofa continue the avian and seafaring theme.

TOP AND ABOVE The narrow wooden staircase winds up from the hall, taking minimal space between an original fitted cupboard and the door to the bathroom. At the top, a small landing opens onto two bedrooms at the front and one at the back.

Ramiro Fernandez Saus and Anthea Craigmyle, whose art classes Victoria attended, as well as a couple by Victoria herself: a portrait of their dog Daisy and a small seascape on a piece of wood she found on the beach.

Ships, shells, seabirds and the sea are a theme throughout. Downstairs there are framed models of sailing ships and ships in bottles. Upstairs there are sailors' valentines, exquisite baskets and bouquets of flowers sculpted from tiny shells, not made by the sailors themselves but brought back as presents for loved ones after long voyages. Victoria is the sort of person who could make a sailor's valentine herself – and she has sailed the Atlantic in a crew of six. After a successful career as a television presenter, she returned to her talent for art and for making things, and now, when not out on the water, she runs creative workshops. She and Edward are generous supporters of the Pallant House Gallery in Chichester, among other arts-related and charitable causes, as well as sailing together. 'But when it comes to furnishing and decorating,' says Victoria, 'he leaves it to me. He knows how much I love it.'

OPPOSITE AND ABOVE Victoria chose the Tess Newall Herbarium wallpaper with its large-scale sprigs to give the main bedroom 'a doll's house feel'. The painted wooden bed is from Tobias and the Angel and was chosen for its height, which brings the mattress to the level of the front window such that you can see the view from the bed. The bedspread is an antique patchwork and two early 19th-century sailors' valentines hang on the wall, above the bed and the dressing table.

LEFT The house is visited far less often by the family in winter, when Victoria says they all 'run in and out of the downstairs bathroom and back to bed or the fire to get warm'.

THIS PAGE The second bedroom at the front of the cottage has an equally elevated bed and above its fireplace another nautical painting by Ramiro Fernandez Saus that echoes the view from these upstairs front windows of moonlight reflected in the sea. The 'V' on the deck is a Roman numeral rather than 'V' for Victoria. There are also two ships in bottles, a cased sailing ship and shell-framed valentines.

OPPOSITE The bedroom at the back is where all three children slept as they grew up and spent summers here learning to sail, the youngest of them occupying the Victorian metal cot bed. All the floors upstairs are painted boards. 'So much more practical for sandy feet than fitted carpet,' says Victoria.

THIS PAGE Victoria and Edward's children, now adults, still sleep in the pair of Victorian metal beds in the back bedroom, the right-hand one beneath a vintage hanging from Victoria's childhood bedroom. The two cushions with appliquéd dogs belonged to her mother and aunt, and the woolwork of a ship is by Colin Millington.

REPAIR SHOP

Tim Smith is not a man to be put off by a bit of wear and tear. His 18th-century cherrywood dining chairs had elm seats riddled with woodworm, his Georgian sofa had broken rails and sagging upholstery and his terraced townhouse on a side alley in Ludlow, Shropshire had rotten windows, a sapling growing out of a top-floor bedroom and a hole in the roof that leaked water into a downstairs cupboard, filling the ground-floor kitchen with up to 15cm/six inches of water. 'The previous tenant, who had a photocopy shop here, said to me "For heaven's sake don't buy it, the place is a nightmare."'

ABOVE LEFT AND BELOW The shop is down a side alley just off the central market square. The name Mackenzie on the frontage refers to Tim's former business partner, also a furniture restorer, with whom he used to share premises.

BELOW RIGHT Pieces of furniture restored and for sale are displayed in the windows, as is a 19th-century cabinetmaker's end vice.

OPPOSITE Tim lives in rooms behind and above his workshop in the middle of Ludlow and can often be seen at his bench through the quaintly bowed pair of shop windows on either side of his door from the street. He is a furniture restorer and prefers to work with old and often antique woodworking tools, some of which are clustered, wooden handles upwards, along the back of his bench.

THIS PAGE A door at the back of the workshop leads directly to the stairs and the kitchen, which looks onto a small courtyard. The painted wooden fire surround and mantel is a recent addition, found 'on a bit of rough land behind the supermarket' and restored by Tim.

BUT ONE MAN'S NIGHTMARE is another man's ideal home. 'I loved it,' says Tim. 'Its core is 17th century, but it was "modernized" at the turn of the 19th century, and the ground floor made an ideal space for my workshop.' Tim is a furniture restorer, sought after by antiques dealers and private clients for his impeccable craftsmanship and respect for patina. Behind the pot-bellied shop windows on either side of the front door there is a workbench bristling with the old wooden-handled tools he prefers to work with, while the space opposite is stacked floor to ceiling with grandfather clocks, chests, tables and chairs, all awaiting his attentions.

If you come as a guest rather than as a client you will be invited to take a narrow path between the workbench and the furniture, through a door and past the wooden stairs to the kitchen, which looks onto a small courtyard surrounded by adjacent buildings and overlooked by the church tower. 'There's still an outdoor privy,' says Tim, 'but you have to keep the door shut, otherwise, as I found to my cost, visitors climbing the church tower have a view straight in.'

Tim tells a good story, with a dry sense of humour, whether relating how a friend compared the kitchen to 'Tutankhamun's tomb' or how a

BELOW Tableware is stored in the pine dresser/hutch to the left of the fireplace, and the kitchen table with its scrubbed pine top is just big enough to accommodate six chairs. The oxblood linoleum was the end of a roll and reminds Tim of his prep school. Simple wooden stairs lead up to the first-floor living room, dining room, Tim's bedroom and the bathroom.

LEFT When Tim first came here, there was one single room above the workshop. From this, he has created two rooms, a dining room and a living room, by dividing the space with a wall of reclaimed 18th-century panelling and a salvaged door of a similar period.

ABOVE AND OPPOSITE All the furniture in the dining room has been restored by Tim and is 18th century, except for the late 17th-century caned chair just seen to the right of the door into the living room. Grandfather clocks are among Tim's favourite projects, and this room has two. The plate rack had been stored in a chicken shed and used as a roost.

girlfriend left him for prioritizing a new chimneypiece over installing central heating, even when it was so cold the butter froze. 'I did get round to it eventually,' he says. 'I have four radiators – but only for emergency use.' One of his best stories is how he decided to train as a furniture restorer, the result of being abandoned by a previous girlfriend in a cave on a Greek island where they were eking a living on the proceeds of her skill braiding hair. 'She left me for a woman she had been having a relationship with who turned up unannounced. I only had 30p, so she taught me how to braid and I earned enough to get home. It made me realize I could make a living by learning a craft. I had always loved antiques – I started

OPPOSITE Making a suitable chimneypiece for the living room fireplace was a priority for Tim – more important than installing central heating. He still only has a few radiators, so the fire is an important source of warmth.

RIGHT An 18th-century corner cupboard with its original green-painted interior and pretty gothic glazing bars is bursting with 18th- and early 19th-century china, including Delft plates, two Staffordshire cow creamers, pearlware and creamware. The candlestick figures are 18th-century Derby and were 'ludicrously cheap'.

PAGES 148–149 Tim bought the 18th-century sofa at auction and brought it home sticking out of the back of his van. It had lost its middle supporting legs and needed new webbing, but he managed to save its 1950s cherry-red velvet instead of replacing it.

collecting things, mostly scavenged, when I was a boy and filled my bedroom with them – so antique furniture really appealed.'

He continues to scavenge and has just fitted a splendid Victorian chimneypiece round his Aga range cooker, which he found 'on some rough ground behind Tesco'. Other recent additions are the 1930s brass light switches, bought as a job lot in a shoebox for £10. Also in the kitchen is a grandfather clock, one of several presiding over these

small rooms, that he 'rescued from dereliction'. Here, as elsewhere, there are large pieces of antique furniture – a table and six chairs, and a cupboard with glazed doors – that seem to defy the lack of space.

Winding up the stairs, you discover Tim has applied the same principle to the rooms above the shop. His bedroom over the kitchen at the back is filled by a Victorian brass bedstead, with just enough room to open the door. He has kept the old fittings in the bathroom

LEFT AND ABOVE Tim's bedroom is on the first floor above the kitchen and contains an antique brass bed, a chair and a chest of drawers, plus one of four radiators in the house for 'emergencies and guests'. The view through the open door is across the landing and into the dining room beyond.

RIGHT AND BELOW RIGHT Looking back across the landing from the dining room to the bedroom with the door to the bathroom on the right. Tim kept the original fittings and mended the lavatory cistern. Bathroom walls are Farrow & Ball Pavilion Blue, and the floor is oxblood red linoleum like the kitchen.

next to it, having lined the cistern with fibreglass. At the front is his 'dining room', which mainly consists of a 'really good' George II table and the cherrywood dining chairs. Next door is his equally diminutive living room, which in turn is dominated by a splendidly capacious 1.8-metre/6-foot Georgian sofa.

'A lot of my furniture comes and goes,' Tim says. 'The dining table is only temporary, as I have sold it to a friend. But the sofa is something I wouldn't let go. I bought it from a picture in an auction catalogue and brought it home hanging out of the back of my van. I had to make new rails and supporting legs for it, and put in new webbing, which meant taking off and putting back the 1950s upholstery. It took me and my assistant Martin a whole morning getting it up the stairs and hauling it over the banisters. It was awful. But instead of making a room feel smaller, a few substantial pieces seem to have quite the opposite effect.'

THIS PAGE AND OPPOSITE On the second floor above the living room there is a guest bedroom, also with an antique brass bedstead and a small wing chair covered in vintage linen tucked into the corner. Tim says his cat is 'very sensible' and always finds the best spots – on top of the Aga or on a chair next to the living room fire in winter, and a cooler resting place by an open window in summer.

ARTISTS IN RESIDENCE

In 1972, aged eight, Marion drew a picture of her black cat that was published in The Beano *comic magazine. She still has a copy, its paper slightly yellowed with age – a cat with character, a bit skew-whiff, front legs akimbo, tail oddly fat. 'It's the first time I was published,' she says, 'and I distinctly remember being hugely proud of how photo-real it was!' Now an artist, illustrator, teacher and author with a huge body of work behind her, including prints, books, greetings cards, tea towels, packaging and mugs, Marion still has a black cat and shares a cottage just off the market square in a West Midlands market town with him and with her partner Neil, who teaches art and design. Their daughter Stella studied neuroscience and is now working in London.*

THE THREE OF THEM moved here from London 20 years ago when Neil was offered a teaching post at Birmingham City University. 'It was a long commute,' says Marion, 'but this area seemed like a groovy place with its arts centre and Michelin-starred restaurants. In London we had shared ownership of a ground-floor maisonette. Here we rented and it felt like we had our pockets full and lots of choice. When I first saw this house, I wanted to live in it. We offered, and got turned down, but they came back

ABOVE LEFT The front door is just inside the entrance to an alley off a narrow side street and opens directly into the kitchen, which was once used as an inn. There are three more cottages on this side of the alley and three opposite.

LEFT Bottles of herbs and spices and an old postcard of Queen Elizabeth II are lined up on the kitchen mantelpiece.

OPPOSITE The kitchen has minimal storage, which includes old wooden crates screwed to the walls as a 'temporary' measure when Marion and Neil moved in 20 years ago. The fireplace still encloses the Victorian range cooker and the glass-fronted cabinet hanging above it contains a mix of things collected over the years, including vintage tins, bottles and wooden rulers.

to us six months later. It was such a novelty to have our own staircase – two, in fact – and to have space that wasn't entirely necessary.'

You can see why Marion fell for it, though 'space' and 'necessary' are relative terms. Just inside an alley on a street so narrow vans and lorries sometimes catch the corner of the 17th-century jettied first floor, the front door opens into a neat little beamed kitchen. Stairs so steep you almost crawl up them are squashed into a corner by the window onto the street and bring you to a landing that is the living room. The three other cottages along this side and sitting at right

ABOVE In pride of place on a chest of drawers in the corner of the kitchen is a Staffordshire flatback figure of Queen Victoria as a young woman. The painting is by a friend of Marion's mother. The Toby jug on the left depicts Lord Kitchener and the one on the right came from Marion's grandfather's pub.

RIGHT With a window onto the alley to the left of the fireplace and a window onto the street, the kitchen is the only room on the ground floor. A tight curl of steep stairs leads up from the corner next to the front window to the living room above, which is a foot or so bigger thanks to the jetty that protrudes over the street.

angles to the road have just single rooms stacked one above the other on three floors. This one has the advantage of extra rooms that form a bridge over the entrance – a tiny first-floor bathroom and study, and above them Stella's bedroom. The main bedroom has exactly the same footprint as the living room and kitchen below it. Compact but charming, with pretty sash windows and the slightly crooked appeal of Marion's cat in *The Beano.*

Originally built to house the workers who serviced the many grand townhouses nearby, these cottages and the ones on the other side of the alley were condemned as unfit for habitation as recently as the 1990s. They were rescued by a housing association, restored and given indoor bathrooms.

'We did nothing structural when we moved in,' says Marion, 'just filled it with our stuff and did things like hang some wooden crates on the kitchen wall to use as temporary shelf and cupboard space, and then never replaced them.'

Both Neil and Marion are collectors. The walls throughout are busy with pictures, many of them by friends including the artist Delaine Le Bas, and shelves are double stacked with books. Marion's love of folk culture, typography, mottos and religious iconography is reflected in the groups of Staffordshire flatback figures, old china decorated with names and sayings, an assortment of coronation mugs, colourful framed posters, images of circuses and fairgrounds, and horse brasses.

OPPOSITE AND ABOVE Marion's collection of antique and vintage china, mostly bought from local flea and antiques markets, is displayed on wall shelves and the top of the chest of drawers in the kitchen. The collection includes coronation and commemorative mugs, old glass bottles and a Welsh money box with cotton-reel bow windows. Marion is attracted to folk art and china with mottos, such as the Sunderland lustreware mug (opposite, top left) with its 'Sailors Farewell'.

ABOVE LEFT The stairs from the kitchen climb so steeply you find yourself using your hands for balance. A door under the stairs leads down to a cellar that would have been in use when the house was an inn. The back of the door is the family coat rack.

THIS PAGE The drawers of the plan chest in the living room open to reveal the glorious colours of original works by Marion. Pictures above it include two more abstracts by her mother's friend. Two chairs face the sofa, one with a cushion in a fabric by Marimekko.

OPPOSITE BELOW The stairs between the kitchen and living room are open such that the sofa back is against the banister rail. Every available corner is used for storage, here a slimline bookcase. Linocuts and engravings, mostly by friends, hang above the stairs and include a lady with a plume of feathers in her hat inscribed 'for Marion' by artist Chris Brown.

Several feet of shelving in the bedroom are devoted to Neil's jazz records, neatly arranged in alphabetical order, and a smaller bookcase by the bed is full of his vintage paperbacks, bought for the artwork on their covers. Cricket is represented by an oval mirror frame made by Neil and decorated with raised papier-mâché mouldings and the names of famous partnerships, among them his own with his brother-in-law, which commemorates when they scored a century. Also more Neil than Marion are the pictures of aeroplanes,

THIS PAGE In the living room there are ceramics by Marion in the fireplace, and her patchwork cushions on the sofa and chair, while the mirror frame and papier-mâché cowboy head are both by Neil. Marion bought the print over the chest of drawers for its frame, only to discover that it looks perfectly at home here.

TOP The house has a particularly powerful sense of family and friends, as so many of its furnishings are their creations. Neil embellished the mirror over the fireplace by applying papier mâché to its wooden frame and painting it with the names of celebrated cricketing partnerships to mark an occasion when he and Marion's brother made a century.

ABOVE The plan chest on the right of the living-room fireplace is full of original artworks by Marion. Her fabulous sense of colour and design has been translated into prints and posters, book illustrations, greetings cards and packaging, and can also be seen in the rooms of her house.

LEFT This is the largest cottage in the row thanks to the rooms above the entrance to the alley, which are reached through a curtained doorway from the living room. At the beginning of the last century, the house belonged to the town lamplighter who brought up 13 children here. The door ahead is an understairs cupboard and the window looks up the alley. The bathroom is on the left slotted between the landing and Neil's study, which overlooks the street.

BELOW This second staircase leads up to the second-floor landing, seen here from the main bedroom. The staircase wall is hung with three vintage film posters, the lowest one designed by Ronald Searle for the film *Blue Murder at St Trinian's*.

OPPOSITE Shelves above a delightfully battered bedside cupboard hold more of Marion's treasured collection of Staffordshire flatback figures and a pair of greyhounds. The collage above is by Marion. 'It's that *Beano* cat again,' she says.

and two collages made using the backs of stamps by artist Dan Fern. These as well as other artworks in Neil's study are from an exhibition entitled *Pushing the Envelope*, which he devised and curated to commemorate the 175th anniversary of the first postage stamp. Talking to Neil about the history of the postal service is to find yourself fascinated, perhaps for the first time, by stamp collecting.

Last year Marion's mother died. She and Marion's father had owned a bookshop in Liverpool where they hosted poetry evenings and had friendships with many writers and artists. Like Marion and Neil, they were collectors. Many of their paintings and hundreds of their books have somehow found a place in these rooms already so rich with art and interest. 'We just had to move things round a bit,' says Marion.

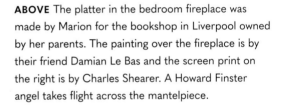

ABOVE The platter in the bedroom fireplace was made by Marion for the bookshop in Liverpool owned by her parents. The painting over the fireplace is by their friend Damian Le Bas and the screen print on the right is by Charles Shearer. A Howard Finster angel takes flight across the mantelpiece.

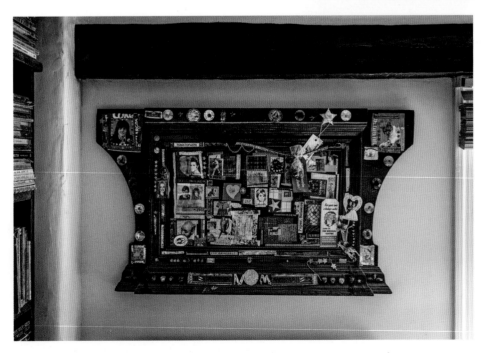

ABOVE AND LEFT As well as stamps, which are stored in his office, and vinyl jazz records, ranked in shelves at the end of the bed, Neil has a collection of vintage paperback novels from the 1940s and '50s that he loves for the artwork on the covers. The artwork to the left of the window was commissioned some years ago by Neil from artists Jill and Alan Tattersall as a present for Marion and incorporates old photos, holiday souvenirs, a favourite cat's collar and pictures of Elvis and Donny Osmond.

OPPOSITE AND PAGES 168–169 The two paintings propped on an easel at the end of the bed are views of Liverpool by Clifford Fishwick. Marion and Neil bought the bed when they lived in London and the only way they could get it into the house was to saw it in half and reassemble it in situ. Unlike the living-room sofa, it wouldn't fit through the front window.

CITY ROMANCE

Half-an-hour's walk south from the National Theatre, the district of Walworth is home to a pioneering housing estate for working-class Londoners built at the end of the 19th century by social reformer and joint founder of the National Trust, Octavia Hill. Central though it is, the area has a leafy, airy feel, the wide streets lined with pretty brick cottages. Many have twin front doors, one for each of the ground-floor and first-floor flats, and some are arranged around central allotments accessed through a gate from their backyards.

THE CONVENIENT LOCATION, a front door of his own, a private backyard and the potential for an allotment (there is a short waiting list) were all big attractions for Kevin Oliver. 'I had been renting since I first came to London naively hoping to find a job in the art world,' he says. 'I'm an Irish farmer, brought up milking cows in County Mayo. I studied Classics and History of Art at Trinity, Dublin and imagined the streets of London were paved with gold. I quickly realized I couldn't earn a decent living at an auction house, so decided I could turn the discipline of a History degree to the moving of commas writing documents for a financial institution.' Further questioning reveals that he then did a Master of Laws alongside a full-time job. Disarmingly self-effacing, Kevin describes his work as 'in financial services', and you can't help suspecting he is more high-powered than he cares to admit.

OPPOSITE The living room is the first on the right leading off the entrance hall and has a period cast-iron chimneypiece and good ceiling height. The tall 18th-century mirror over the fireplace emphasizes the height and is appropriately Irish. It has lost all its gilding, leaving the smooth coating of gesso on the carved wood, and was found by Kevin's chosen interior designer, Carlos Garcia.

ABOVE RIGHT Every ground-floor flat in the terrace has a backyard with a gate opening into a central square of allotments.

RIGHT The curtains are Kandili, and the sofa is covered in Castille, both from the Carlos Garcia Collection. The rug is a vintage Touros nomad kilim found on one of Carlos's trips to Istanbul. Walls are in Persian by Edward Bulmer.

LEFT Carlos persuaded Kevin that a sofa was essential despite the limited floor space and was proved right. There is still space here for two armchairs and a central tray table. 'Furniture has to work hard in a small room,' says Carlos, who chose pieces such as the 17th-century chest of drawers for storage capacity as well as good looks.

ABOVE The bookcase is bespoke from Carlos Garcia, its design based on a George II library cabinet. It is painted in Farrow & Ball Mahogany with bright blue shelves and interior in Azurite from Edward Bulmer. The paintings on either side are from Tat London, and the armchair is upholstered in a vintage kilim.

The flat is small but well-proportioned; a long, narrow entrance hall with a first door to the right opening into a tight square of living room and a second into a bedroom with a window onto the yard. Ahead is the kitchen and, beyond it, the bathroom. Kevin also liked the Arts and Crafts feel of the architecture, although this had been diluted by plastic windows at the back, blocked-in fireplaces and an all-over porridge of woodchip wallpaper.

'Initially, because of its small scale, and because I know what I like, I thought I would do it up myself. I decided to live in it for a while, and resist making it tolerable, so I wouldn't be tempted not to do it properly.

LEFT AND BELOW The long entrance hall leads from the front door to the kitchen past the wall of the stairs to the first-floor flat and with doors to the living room and the bedroom off to the right. Carlos opened up the space under the stairs to make a shelf with curtained shelving beneath and papered it in Colefax and Fowler Citron Squiggle wallpaper to complement the walls in Edward Bulmer Olympian Green.

OPPOSITE After the plain walls of the hall corridor, the kitchen bursts into flower with William Morris Hawthorn Autumn wallpaper. The ebonized rush-seated Sussex chairs are also a William Morris design and were bought from Miles Griffiths Antiques.

PAGES 176 AND 177 The kitchen woodwork, window and cupboards are in mustard yellow Chanterelle from Fenwick & Tilbrook, while the extractor hood is in bright Bluebird from Paint and Paper Library. Bespoke Delft tiles by Douglas Watson Studio wrap around the walls above the cooker, which is in red enamel, while the green kettle picks up another colour from the wallpaper. The table is one of the few pieces Kevin brought with him that survived Carlos's strict edit, though he did have the legs painted in Can-Can from Fenwick & Tilbrook, while the bespoke seagrass rug is by Seagrass Story. The door to the right leads to the bathroom and the back door into the rear courtyard.

But work became incredibly busy, and I realized I needed help. A friend recommended Pinterest and that was where I saw a picture of Carlos's [Garcia's] pantry. It had a layered, old-fashioned feel and something of the romance of the old stone cottages in Ireland that all the farmers moved out of as soon as they could afford to build a bungalow. I loved them as a boy and still do.'

By this time Kevin had lived in the flat for 18 months. 'One evening, I took my courage in my hands and emailed Carlos. I didn't think a decorator of his calibre would touch such a tiny project with a bargepole, but I dangled Octavia Hill as a carrot, closed my eyes and pressed "send". A couple of days later, Carlos replied and said he would come to see me the next Wednesday. I was astonished.' For his part, Carlos was intrigued by the modesty of the proposal. 'I realized that something this small would need particularly careful design,' he says. 'It was a mess, but we sat down and started talking, and haven't stopped since!'

Kevin wanted colour, pattern and for the flat to feel like an interior that had evolved over time. The finished rooms have all this in abundance, and a joyful, cosy atmosphere. His existing furnishings were few, aside from books and some pictures, including a collage by his friend the award-winning illustrator George Butler, which now hangs in the hall. Furniture was chosen to be functional as well as beautiful. 'We had to maximize storage,' says Carlos, 'every piece had to work for its place.' He persuaded Kevin that a sofa was essential – 'somewhere to flop after a hard day at the office' – and proved the truth of the decorating adage that large pieces, carefully placed, make a small room seem bigger.

OPPOSITE The cupboard to the left of the sink hides the wall-mounted boiler. Inside its door is a spice rack. Curtains in Suffolk Check by Ian Mankin hide the dishwasher and washing machine, and the window curtains are Iridee Blue by Aleta Fabrics.

ABOVE AND RIGHT A square of back hall separates the kitchen from the back door and opens into the bathroom. The chequerboard terracotta tiling was one of the few remaining original features in the flat. Carlos added the panelling and painted it in Red Squirrel from Fenwick & Tilbrook to pick up the colour of the tiles. The curtain is Little Chintz Olive, another design by William Morris.

PAGES 180 AND 181 Carlos found reclaimed floor tiles at English Salvage to match the floor of the back hall and placed the washbasin under the window with a mirror hung over it to make best use of the space. The period-style basin is from Burlington Bathrooms and the bathtub is from Victorian Plumbing. Doorknobs here and throughout the flat are old-fashioned Bakelite from Broughtons of Leicester and the walls are papered in Sadras Verd de Pomme from Nicole Fabre Designs.

In addition to the sofa, the living room accommodates a freestanding bookcase, an early 17th-century chest of drawers, an 18th-century supper table with drawers, two armchairs and three occasional tables. It's snug, and very comfortable.

The bedroom is a bower of chintz – walls, curtains, upholstery, bedhead – all dancing with yellow hibiscus flowers. The kitchen is similarly flower-powered, here with a William Morris paper. But there's a lot going on behind the eye-candy. Hung inside the door of the boiler cupboard door is a neat little spice rack. Gingham curtains hide the dishwasher and washing machine, and there is a larder cupboard slotted under the stairs of the upstairs flat. 'I believe in the power of good design to improve people's lives,' says Carlos. Octavia Hill did too.

ABOVE In the bedroom, like the kitchen, the all-over pattern of Hibiscus Saffron wallpaper from Carlos's own fabric collection is a visual surprise after the plain walls outside its door.

ABOVE LEFT, LEFT AND OPPOSITE The wrap-around pattern is intensified by the use of matching Hibiscus chintz on the headboard, chair and curtains and pelmet. The fireplace was made for the room by Carlos's joiner and painted in Caspian from Fenwick & Tilbrook. Two handsome pieces of antique furniture hold clothes, an Irish George III mahogany chest of drawers and a 19th-century mahogany linen press, which, unusually, is deep enough to take modern clothes hangers.

SOURCES

ARCHITECTURAL SALVAGE

Lassco
Brunswick House
30 Wandsworth Road
London SW8 2LG
+ 44 (0)20 7394 2100
www.lassco.co.uk
A huge stock of everything from fireplaces to floors to stained glass, panelling and staircases, plus some furniture and pictures. Visit their website for details of their branches in Bermondsey and Oxfordshire.

Oak Beam UK
Ermin Farm
Cricklade Road
Cirencester
Gloucestershire GL7 5PN
+ 44 (0)1285 869 222
www.oakbeamuk.com
Reclaimed oak beams salvaged from Britain and France.
www.oldoakfloor.com
Antique oak floor boards from France.

Norfolk Reclaim Ltd
Helhoughton Road
Fakenham
Norfolk NR21 7DY
+ 44 (0)1328 864743
www.norfolkreclaim.co.uk
Reclaimed building materials including bricks, pantiles and paving, plus architectural antiques and furnishings.

Retrouvius
1016 Harrow Road
London NW10 5NS
+44 (0)20 8960 6060
www.retrouvius.com
Fabulous stock of reclaimed and repurposed antique and vintage furnishings and fittings.

Wells Reclamation
Coxley Wells
Somerset BA5 1RQ
+ 44 (0)1749 677087
www.wellsreclamation.com
Five and a half acres of architectural salvage, reclaimed building materials, antique and vintage furnishings.

BATHROOMS

Antique Bathrooms of Ivybridge
Erme Bridge Works
Ermington Road
Ivybridge
Devon PL21 9DE
+44 (0)1752 698250
www.antiquebaths.com
Reconditioned antique bathtubs plus reproduction ranges.

Balineum
www.balineum.co.uk
Online bathroom fittings and accessories and a choice of pretty hand-painted tiles.

C P Hart
+44 (0)20 79025250
www.cphart.co.uk
Inspiring bathroom showrooms.

Stiffkey Bathrooms
89 Upper St Giles Street
Norwich NR2 1AB
+44 (0)1603 627850
www.stiffkeybathrooms.com
Antique sanitaryware plus their own range of reproduction bathroom accessories.

The Water Monopoly
The Honey Factory
London NW10 6QU
+44 (0)20 7624 2636
www.thewatermonopoly.com
Opulent period baths, basins, and fittings.

FABRICS

Bennison Fabrics
16 Holbein Place
London SW1W 8NL
+44 (0)20 7730 8076
www.bennisonfabrics.com
Chintzes, florals, stripes and damasks inspired by antique originals.

Chelsea Textiles
13 Walton Street
London SW3 2HX
+44 (0)20 7584 5544
www.chelseatextiles.com
Embroidered cottons, delicate prints, linens, silks and voiles with a distinctly 18th- century feel.

Colefax and Fowler
110 Fulham Road
London SW3 6HU
+44 (0)20 7244 7427
www.colefax.com
Quintessentially English fabrics and wallpapers.

GP & J Baker
Unit 10 Ground Floor
Design Centre East
Chelsea Harbour
London SW10 OXF
+44 (0)20 7351 7760
www.gpjbaker.co.uk
Fabrics both traditional and contemporary.

Ian Mankin
269/271 Wandsworth Bridge Road
London SW6 2TX
+44 (0)20 7722 0997
www.ianmankin.co.uk
Natural fabrics, including unbleached linens, butter muslin and striped tickings.

Lewis & Wood
105–106 First Floor
Design Centre East
Chelsea Harbour
London SW10 0XF
+44 (0)20 7751 4554
www.lewisandwood.co.uk
At the grander end of decorating, with large-scale fabrics and wallpapers.

Robert Kime
190–192 Ebury Street
London SW1 W8U
+44 (0)20 7831 6066
www.robertkime.com
Best of British decorators in the English style, with a gorgeous range of fabrics and wallpapers, and a selection of antiques.

Russell & Chapple
30-31 Store Street
London WC1E 7QE
+44 (0)20 7836 7521
www.randc.net
Artist's canvas in various weights, jutes, muslin, deckchair canvas, and hessian sacking.

Susan Deliss
www.susandeliss.com
Gorgeous bespoke fabrics, including antique and exotic embroideries, cushions and ikat lampshades.

Tinsmiths
8a High Street
Ledbury
Herefordshire HR8 1DS
+44 (0)1531 632083
www.tinsmiths.co.uk
Handwoven and printed textiles, including washed linens, African indigo cottons and Indian block prints, plus lighting, studio ceramics, blankets and cushions.

Thornback & Peel
www.thornbackandpeel.co.uk
Fresh screen-printed cottons, including their instantly recognizable 'Pigeon and Jelly', 'Pea Pod' and 'Rabbit and Cabbage' designs.

ANTIQUE FABRICS

Katharine Pole
+44 (0)774 761 6692
www.katharinepole.com
Wonderful selection of antique textiles, including toiles, plain linens and stripes.

Susy Stirrup
Instagram: @susystirrup
Online decorative antiques and textiles, including quilts, samplers and embroideries.

Francesca Gentilli
The Rug Barn
Lannock Manor
Weston
Hertfordshire SG4 7EE
+44 (0)7779 660690
www.francescagentilli.com
Rugs, cushions, Indian embroideries and throws from all over the world including suzanis.

Su Mason
su.mason@yahoo.co.uk
Lovely selection of French antique linens, workwear and textiles, by appointment, London

FITTINGS

Brass Foundry Castings
+44 (0)1424 845551
www.brasscastings.co.uk
More than 800 brass and foundry castings for furniture, doors and clocks reproduced from 17th- to 20th-century originals, available online or mail order only.

Clayton Munroe
+44 (0)1803 865700
www.claytonmunroe.com
Traditional handles, iron hinges and latches. Mail order only.

FURNITURE– contemporary

The Conran Shop
6 Sloane Square
London SW1W 8ER
+44 (0)207 589 7401
www.conranshop.co.uk
Tasteful modern furniture and accessories that mix well with antiques and look good in older buildings.

Heal's
196 Tottenham Court Road
London W1T 7LQ
+44 (0)20 7636 1666
and branches www.heals.com
Good-quality contemporary furniture.

MADE
www.made.com
Online store selling a range of contemporary furniture sourced directly from the makers.

OKA
www.okadirect.com
Good-quality, mid-price furnishings in classic, contemporary and traditional styles.

SCP
135-139 Curtain Road
London EC2A 3BX
+44 (0)20 7739 1869
www.scp.co.uk
Manufacturer and retailer of the work of contemporary British designers, including Matthew Hilton.

FURNITURE – antique, vintage and traditional

After Noah
261 King's Road
London SW3 5EL
+44 (0)207 3512610
www.afternoah.com
An appealing mix of antique, vintage and contemporary furnishings, including iron beds, lighting and toys.

Alfies Antiques Market
13–25 Church Street
London NW8 8DT
+44 (0)20 7723 6066
www.alfiesantiques.com
Vintage, retro and antique furnishings and a good source of mid-century modern.

Bed Bazaar
The Old Station
Station Road
Framlingham
Suffolk IP13 9EE
+44 (0)1728 723756
www.bedbazaar.co.uk
Antique metal and wooden beds and handmade mattresses to order.

Berdoulat
8 Margaret's Buildings
Bath BA1 2LP
Specialists in period buildings and restoration projects, with a small range of kitchenware, tableware, decorative products and bespoke furniture.

The French House
The Warehouse
North Lane
Huntington
York YO32 9SU
+44 (0)1904 400561
www.thefrenchhouse.co.uk
All manner of French antiques, from armoires to birdcages and bathtubs.

George Smith
589 Kings Road
London SW6 2EH
+44 (0)20 7384 1004
www.georgesmith.com
Capacious and relaxed traditional sofas and armchairs.

Joanna Booth Antiques
+44 (0)20 7352 8998
www.joannabooth.co.uk
Early and rare antiques including sculpture and tapestries.

Max Rollitt
Yavington Barn
Lovington Lane
Avington
Hampshire SO21 1DA
+44 (0)1962 791124
www.maxrollit.com
*(Showroom open by appointment only)
Fine antiques as well as bespoke furniture design.*

Robert Young Antiques
68 Battersea Bridge Road
London SW11 3AG
+44 (0)20 7228 7847
www.robertyoungantiques.com
Fine English furniture and folk art.

Spencer Swaffer Antiques
30 High Street
Arundel
West Sussex BN18 9AB
+44 (0)1903 882132
www.spencerswaffer.com
Pretty shop with glamorous stock.

Wessex Beds
The Old Glove Works
Percombe
Near Stoke-sub-Hamdon
Somerset TA14 6RD
+44 (0)1935 829147
www.wessexbeds.co.uk
Antique beds, including old brass and metal bedsteads.

FLOORING

Alternative Flooring Company
www.alternativeflooring.com
Coir, sea-grass, sisal, jute and wool floor coverings.

Bernard Dru Oak
www.oakfloor.co.uk
Specialists in the supply and installation of English oak flooring and parquet design, made from wood from the company's own woodlands.

Crucial Trading
www.crucial-trading.com
All types of natural floorings, most of which can also be ordered as rugs bound with cotton, linen or leather.

Delabole Slate
www.delaboleslate.co.uk
Riven slate or slate slabs quarried in Cornwall and suitable for work surfaces, fireplaces and flooring.

Farnham Antique Carpets
The Old Parsonage
Church Street
Crondall
Surrey GY10 5QQ
44 (0)1252 851215
www.farnhamantiquecarpets.com
Antique rug specialists offering a full service including restoration and advice, plus a big selection of rugs for sale.

Robert Stephenson and Giuseppe Giannini
1 Elystan Street
London SW3 3NT
44 (0)20 7225 2343
www.robertstephenson.co.uk
Antique rugs from all over the world, including a lovely selection of kilims, plus a specialist restoration and valuation service.

Roger Oates Design
www.rogeroates.com
Natural floorings plus flatweave rugs and runners in chic stripes of gorgeous colour combinations.

Rush Matters
www.rushmatters.co.uk
Rush matting made with English rushes, also baskets and rush seating for chairs.

Solid Floor
61 Paddington Street
London W1U 4JD
+44 (0)20 7486 4838
www.solidfloor.co.uk
Quality wooden floors made from sustainable timber.

Woodworks by Ted Todd
London Design Centre
79 Margaret Street
London W1W 8TA
+44 (0)20 7495 6706
www.woodworksbytedtodd.com
Reclaimed, new, and antique timber flooring and joinery.

HEATING

Jamb
95–97 Pimlico Road
London SW1W 8PH
+ 44 (0)20 7730 2122
and at
8525 Melrose Avenue
West Hollywood
CA 90069, USA
+1 310 315 3028
High-quality reproduction antique fireplaces, also antique fireplaces, reproduction lighting, and an extremely smart selection of antique furnishings.

The Windy Smithy
+44 (0)7866 241783
www.windysmithy.co.uk
Bespoke woodburning stoves.

FINISHING TOUCHES

Fabulous Vintage Finds
www.fabulousvintagefinds.co.uk
Jess Walton and her husband Simon travel around France finding furniture and decorative items to sell, available online and from pop-up shops and markets.

Pentreath & Hall
57 Lambs Conduit Street
London WC1N 3NB
+44 (0)20 7430 2526
www.pentreath-hall.com
Irresistible homewares.

Perfect English Stuff
www.perfectenglishstuff.com
Blatant self-promotion - online antiques store selling decorative antique and vintage items found by three generations of my family – my mother, Margery Byam Shaw, me and my daughter, Elizabeth Kemp.

Phillips & Cheers
www.phillipsandcheers.com
Pretty cushions and lampshades made using vintage floral fabrics.

Ryder & Hope
30 Broad Street
Lyme Regis
Dorset DT7 3QE
+44 (0)1297 443304
www.ryderandhope.com
Contemporary artisan crafts.

Tat
www.tat-london.co.uk
Lovely online selection of vintage and antique pieces, including metal wall sconces, candlesticks, glass and an interesting selection of pictures.

KITCHENS

deVol Kitchens
36 St John's Square
London EC1V 4JJ
+44 (0)20 3879 7900
www.devolkitchens.co.uk
Handcrafted English kitchens.

Fired Earth
www.firedearth.com
Timeless kitchens and bathrooms; also an excellent range of paint colours.

Plain English
+44 (0)1449 774028
www.plainenglishdesign.co.uk
Elegant wooden kitchens (and other cabinetry) for traditional and period interiors.

PAINT

Edward Bulmer Natural Paint
+44 (0)1544 388 535
www.edwardbulmerpaint.co.uk
Eco-friendly paints in a wonderful selection of historic colours developed by architectural historian and interior designer Edward Bulmer.

Farrow & Ball
+44 (0)1202 876141
www.farrow-ball.com
Unbeatable for subtle paint colours with intriguing names, also papers, primers, limewash and distempers.

Francesca's Paints Ltd
+44 (0)20 7228 7694
www.francescaspaint.com
Traditional limewash, eco-emulsion and chalky emulsion.

Paint and Paper Library
3 Elystan Street
London SW3 3NT
+44 (0)20 7823 7755
www.paintlibrary.co.uk
Excellent quality paint in 180 elegant colours, including innumerable shades of off-white.

Papers and Paints by Patrick Baty
4 Park Walk
London SW10 OAD
+44 (0)20 7352 8626
www.papersandpaints.co.uk
In addition to their own excellent paints, this company will mix any colour to order.

LIGHTING

The English House
www.theenglishhouse.co.uk
Simple, classical light fittings handmade in England.

John Cullen Lighting
561–563 Kings Road
London SW6 2EB
+44 (0)20 7371 5400
www.johncullenlighting.co.uk
*Extensive range of light fittings
as well as a bespoke lighting
design service.*

Vaughan
+44 (0)20 7349 4600
www.vaughandesigns.com
*Comprehensive range of replica
period lighting, from lamps to
sconces to chandeliers.*

Pooky
+44 (0)207 351 3003
www.pooky.com
*Excellent online selection of
well-priced lighting, including
ourdoor lighting, colourful resin
lamp bases and a big range of
pretty lampshades.*

WALLCOVERINGS

Cole & Son Ltd
+44 (0)20 7376 4628
www.cole-and-son.com
*Wonderful wallpapers, from
the traditional to the wacky.*

De Gournay
112 Old Church Street
London SW3 6EP
+44 (0)20 7352 9988
www.degournay.com
*Reproductions of hand-painted
18th-century Chinese wallpapers –
the sort of thing you might use
in a chateau.*

Hamilton Weston Wallpapers
The Studio
11 Townshend Road
Richmond, Surrey TW9 1XH
+44 (0) 20 8940 4850
www.hamiltonweston.com
*Historic, bespoke and original
wallpapers, including wonderful
designs by contemporary artists
Marthe Armitage and Flora Roberts.*

Zardi and Zardi
Podgwell Barn,
Sevenleaze Lane
Edge
Stroud
Gloucestershire GL6 6NJ
+44 (0) 1452 814777
www.zardiandzardi.co.uk
*Fabulous reproduction tapestries,
digitally printed on linen and very
convincing.*

BUSINESS CREDITS

Carlos Garcia Interiors
210 King's Wharf
301 Kingsland Road
London E8 4DS
and
Manor Farmhouse
Church Lane
Baconsthorpe
Holt
Norfolk NR25 6LU
+44 (0)7967 659 115
carlos@carlosgarciainteriors.com
www.carlosgarciainteriors.com
Pages 4, 6–7, 170–183.

Caroline Holdaway Design
+44 (0)20 8341 6525
ch@carolineholdaway.com
www.carolineholdaway.com
*Pages 2–3; 82–95;
192 left and centre.*

The House on Dolphin Street
Interior Design Studio
+44 (0)7870 173103
hello@thehouseondolphinstreet.
com
www.thehouseondolphinstreet.
com
Pages 5, 96–109.

Libby Lord Design
info@libbylorddesign.com
www.libbylorddesign.com
Pages 50–65.

Ludlow Curtain Company
The Stables
Station Drive
Ludlow
Shropshire, SY8 2PQ
+44 (0)1584 875533
ludlowcurtains@hotmail.co.uk

Black Bough
www.blackbough.co.uk

GD Ginger Antiques
5 Corve Street
Ludlow
Shropshire SY8 1DA
gdgingerantiquesludlow.com

**Guy Marshall Furniture
Restoration**
guymarshall88@gmail.com
+44 (0)7901 623562
Pages 24–37.

Simon Martin
@simonmartin_art
Pages 38–49.

Morris Studio
Unit 5
The Energy Centre
Bowling Green Walk
London N1 6AL
info@morrisstudio.co.uk
www.morrisstudio.co.uk
Pages 110–123.

PICTURE CREDITS

1 Ali Kelsey's Somerset home; **2–3** The home of interior designer Caroline Holdaway; **4** The home of Kevin Oliver designed by Carlos Garcia carlosgarciainteriors.com; **5** The home of The House on Dolphin Street designer Russell Loughlan in Deal, Kent; **6–7** The home of Kevin Oliver designed by Carlos Garcia carlosgarciainteriors.com; **8** The home of William and Xavier Le Clerc in Kent; **10–23** Ali Kelsey's Somerset home; **24–37** The home of furniture restorer Guy Marshall in Shropshire; **38–49** The Brighton home of Simon Martin, Director of Pallant House Gallery; **50–65** The home of Ludlow interior designer Libby Lord; **66–81** The home of William and Xavier Le Clerc in Kent; **82–95** The home of interior designer Caroline Holdaway; **96–109** The home of The House on Dolphin Street designer Russell Loughlan in Deal, Kent; **110–123** The Barbican home of interior designer Tom Morris, director of Morrisstudio.com; **124–139** The Solent retreat of Victoria and Edward Bonham Carter; **140–153** The home of furniture restorer Tim Smith in Ludlow; **170–183** The home of Kevin Oliver designed by Carlos Garcia carlosgarciainteriors.com; **190–191** The home of William and Xavier Le Clerc in Kent; **192 left and centre** The home of interior designer Caroline Holdaway; **192 right** Ali Kelsey's Somerset home.

INDEX

ACKNOWLEDGMENTS

For the last sixteen years I have worked with peerless photographer and dear friend Jan Baldwin. She was not available for this book, but I was lucky enough to find a superb successor. Antony Crolla has been a joy to work with. He has the greatest eye for beauty and composition – and tells the best anecdotes.

People often ask how I find the locations for a book. Forty years' worth of friendships and contacts helps, and I also have the support of an excellent researcher, Jess Walton. For this book there is one person in particular I have to thank, decorator Libby Lord. Several years ago, Libby told me about her friend Guy Marshall, and another friend with an equally lovely house, Tim Smith. Guy's diminutive mansion was the first inspiration for writing about decorating on a small scale, and he put me in touch with Will Le Clerc. When Libby heard about the book, she suggested her own house might qualify and that of Marion Elliot. A chain of connections that supplied no less than five locations.

A book is a collaboration, and it has been a pleasure as always to work with the team at Ryland Peters and Small. I am grateful for the encouragement and way with words of editor Annabel Morgan, the creative overview of art director Leslie Harrington, the design expertise of Toni Kay and the organizational skills of production manager Gordana Simakovic.